C000039073

Why Mankind Has Needed Religion Whereas Bees Have Not

Religious prescriptions provide
the building blocks for the cultural evolution
of distinct human moral communities

Peter Lachmann

Grosvenor House
Publishing Limited

The right of Peter Lachmann to be identified as the author of this
work has been asserted in accordance with Section 78
of the Copyright, Designs and Patents Act 1988

The book cover is copyright to Peter Lachmann

This book is published by
Grosvenor House Publishing Ltd
Link House
140 The Broadway, Tolworth, Surrey, KT6 7HT.
www.grosvenorhousepublishing.co.uk

A CIP record for this book
is available from the British Library

ISBN 978-1-78623-680-7

This book is dedicated to my wife Sylvia, physician and archaeologist, without whose unfailing help and support it would never have been written.

Foreword

There are still those – religious believers and scientists alike, as well as many members of the public – who think of the relation between evolutionary science and religious commitment as a battle over fundamentals. The great virtue and originality of this brief but weighty essay is that it dismantles such a crude polarisation and provides a genuinely fresh approach, grounded not only in a lifetime of first-class scientific research but also in the experience of keeping bees, and the close observation of natural processes and group behaviour that goes with this. The basic point is that genetics as an explanatory tool will work only at certain levels of organic life. Much can be said about its usefulness at levels of organic life where we don't have to think about culture, narrative, language and so on. But a context in which we *do* have to reckon with the complexities of these phenomena means that genetic fundamentalism will not take us far, and ends up purveying mythologies as startling as some of the religious language it purports to overthrow. Human intelligence – tool-making, language-using, environment-modifying – builds solidarity and co-operation not by bare genetic kinship and triggered moments of genetic recognition but by more cumulative and complex processes. And religion enters into this as a key element in defining shared purpose and enabling a dependable moral environment for agents who have the capacity to reflect on their agency and shape their possibilities together – agents who have rather more factors to absorb than do bees.

This essay is a beautifully lucid and focused account of the issues, and includes a notably clear and magisterial introduction to the basics of genetics that will be readily accessible to the non-scientist. It gives no ground either to dogmatic secularists or to believers ambitious to impose their views on a wider society. There will doubtless be aspects of the argument that a believer will want to challenge or at least qualify substantially. More could be said about the 'mystical' element in religious practice, the cultivation of habits of disciplined openness to the sacred in silence and concentration; and the conclusion that faith needs to operate strictly in a private sphere could be questioned. Many would agree that there can and should be no expectation that religious conviction should dictate public policy, while accepting also that personal conviction inevitably shapes public decision making and has a role in public argument – and that we cannot easily imagine an agent in public or in private who approaches any major issue without certain stories, models and beliefs entering into their judgement. Good public argument is not always a matter simply of setting out neutral and incontrovertible facts alone, but of finding how we hold diverse positions in tension, in a way that is faithful to the world as it is but also makes for sustainable cultural and imaginative exchange, and growth in understanding.

But these queries are indices of the boldness, broad scope and clear-headedness of the case set out. For all its brevity, this is a work capable of contributing something genuinely new to what is often a dialogue of the deaf, and it deserves a very warm welcome.

Rowan Williams
Master of Magdalene College
Cambridge

Introduction

Darwinian (or genetic) evolution accounts very successfully for the evolution of new species over long periods of time, often measured in hundreds of millions of years. This, however, cannot account for the very rapid evolution of human progress since the agricultural revolution, only some 10,000 years ago. During this period, humans have moved from being hunter-gatherers living in small groups, to a situation in which they have made enormous advances in the knowledge of their own origins and background, but have also had major – not always desirable – effects on the world around them. This has been achieved by the process known as 'cultural evolution', which is not dependent on genes. Cultural evolution, however, like Darwinian evolution, requires natural selection; and natural selection requires a mechanism for maintaining patterns of behaviour that are sufficiently constant in a sufficient number of people and over a sufficient period of time that natural selection can operate.

The proposition that is to be defended in this book is that it is religions that provide the building blocks which cultural evolution uses for this purpose. This implies that it is the prescriptions of religions, the 'thou shalts' and the 'though shalt nots' that are the really important aspects of religion from the cultural-evolution point of view.

My interest in thinking about religion as an evolutionary adaptation which has provided the building blocks for the cultural evolution of human moral communities stems from a variety of sources. Firstly, I am an immunologist with a keen interest in infectious disease and am well aware that resisting infection is the true function of our immune system. Infectious disease has throughout history made a far greater impact on human society than is commonly realised. Until the advent of modern public health, vaccination and antibiotics, half of all children born were dead before the age of five and, thereafter, death occurred at a slower but continuous rate, with half of the remaining population being dead by the age of 40 as shown in Figure 1. In contrast, death from natural causes is now uncommon before the age of 60. This early mortality was due predominantly to infectious disease. It is plausible that this extremely high burden of infectious disease in humans may be in some part due to the agricultural revolution some 10,000 years ago when humans began to live in larger groups and at settled sites, and to keep domesticated animals, all of which will have contributed to increased exposure to microorganisms, not least from their own excreta contaminating their water supplies. Various behaviour patterns associated with religious observance, as will be discussed in detail, can be seen to have benefits with regard to infectious disease and therefore to improve life expectancy.

Figure 1 Patterns of Survival (from Cairns 1997)

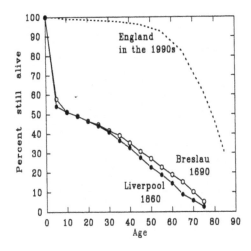

Secondly, I have researched for most of my career the complement system which plays an important role in both innate and acquired immunity. The complement system is remarkably complex and is best understood by considering its evolution. This demonstrates very clearly how the molecular evolution of a 'complex triggered enzyme cascade' (see MacFarlane 1969) is brought about and this example, on its own, is quite sufficient to rule out the idea of 'design', intelligent or otherwise, in explaining molecular evolution. This makes the commonly advanced hypothesis that biological complexity reflects some divine activity quite untenable.

Thirdly, I am a beekeeper. Bee behaviour was quite central to the idea that altruism can be accounted for by recognition of genetic similarity (kin selection) as described by W.D. Hamilton and Richard Dawkins.

However, I will describe why this reflects a fallacious view of bee behaviour.

What is Evolution?

Evolution of the Universe

The idea that the universe was formed within seven days at a time of roughly 4004 BC, according to the calculations of Bishop Usher, is an interpretation of the Book of Genesis. In other religions, such as Hinduism, there are quite incompatible accounts, such as the churning of the ocean of milk. There are numerous other cosmological accounts, such as the Earth is carried on the back of a tortoise, or that it is held up by giants in the Atlas Mountains. It is not possible in the modern world to take any of these accounts as realistic in a scientific sense. They are better referred to as 'creation myths' and reflect the views propounded long ago to deal with the mystery of the Earth and the sky as they were observed by man.

It was probably the ancient Greeks who first looked sceptically at the origins of the universe. However, for the contemporary world, it was Copernicus and Galileo who pointed out that the Earth was not at the centre of even the solar system and that it was the Earth that rotated round the sun rather than the sun rotating round the Earth. While this was rejected fiercely at that time by the Roman Catholic Church, it is rare now to find anyone who would deny this proposition. In the last half a millennium, the origins of the universe have been substantially clarified by enormous advances in cosmology and astrophysics, as described by Stephen Hawking and Leonard Mlodinow in 2011 in their book *The Grand Design*. It is now almost universally accepted that the universe in which we live is around fifteen billion years old and originated during what is now described as 'the big bang', and that it started from a minute source and expanded rapidly. Our own planet Earth is about four and a half billion years old and is one of a number of planets which rotate round a particular star, the sun, which is one of a huge number in our own galaxy. This galaxy in turn is one of a huge number of other galaxies. It is not within my capacity to discuss these cosmological topics in any detail but it is worth pointing out that questions of what, if anything, preceded the big bang are beyond human ability to conceive in any detail. Martin Rees suggested in 2001 that there are multiverses, that ours is only one of a number of universes and that others do, or have, existed; but there is no way, at present, that we can know about them. For the purposes of biological evolution, which I am about to consider, there is therefore no basis for speculating beyond fifteen billion years ago.

The Evolution of Life on Earth

It is also, now, very widely agreed that life on the planet Earth originated some three and a half billion years ago, which is more than half the time for which it has existed. The earliest forms of life achieved the ability to reproduce themselves and to metabolise without photosynthesis and without light, using chemical reactions. It is possible that the Earth was bombarded with organic material from neighbouring planets and possibly with very primitive forms of life early in its history. Nevertheless, it is now apparent that all life as we know it on Earth is derived from a single ancestral source. This does not mean that there was only ever one original form of 'life', only that one form successfully out-competed all the others – every race has a winner. Attempts have been made to model the way in which very primitive organisms may have been formed from a primordial soup containing organic molecules, and various mechanisms have been proposed by Leslie Orgel (1973). There seems little doubt that this is basically what occurred. The subsequent evolution of the various life forms that then evolved is itself a hugely complex topic about which there is a very extensive literature.

What is quite clear is that three and a half billion years ago the life the Earth could support was extremely limited. There was no free oxygen, so animals, such as we know them, could not exist. Furthermore, life probably started where there was very little light. Therefore plants, as we know them, could not originally have existed either. The original forms of life were based on chemosynthetic reactions and indeed the Archaea – early chemosynthetic organisms – have persisted to this day and have been discovered, particularly in deep ocean vents as reported by Takai and Nakamura in 2011. As organic life increased, it began to produce the conditions under which more advanced forms of life could develop. At some stage, the Archaea gave rise to bacteria which continue to exist in hugely multiple forms, and to early 'eukaryotic' life (where cells contain chromosomes). Then, where there was sunlight, probably originally on the surface of the oceans and over long periods of time, the process of photosynthesis was developed whereby plants are able to absorb the sun's energy and to convert carbon dioxide into carbohydrates, thereby liberating free oxygen. These conditions, again over very long periods, allowed animal life to develop. In the Carboniferous age (which occurred 359–299 million years ago) the excess of plant life over animal life was enormous and huge quantities of plant material became buried, giving rise to the coal and oil we have now and which, in more recent years, we have exploited as a source of energy. As animal life developed and became more numerous and much more varied, this balance changed, until in recent centuries there has been much greater consumption of carbohydrate by animals, turning it back to carbon dioxide and water which is causing an increase in levels of carbon dioxide and a growing imbalance between plant and animal life. This is at the basis of our present problems with global warming, and achieving a new balance is going to be essential in the near future.

In spite of the volumes that have been written on this subject there are essentially two solutions to the climate change problem which are necessary and complementary. The first is to reduce the amount of animal life or its consumption of food and resources. The second is to increase the contribution of plant life to the consumption of carbon dioxide, which can be achieved either by increasing the acreage over which plants are grown, or by using modern genetic manipulation to increase the efficiency of photosynthesis as described by Lord Porter of Luddenham in 1995. The latter would not be easy but would be a hugely powerful tool and would enable balance to be restored fairly easily and quickly. A further alternative is to substitute other forms of energy for photosynthesis by plants. These could include nuclear energy and/or tidal, wave or wind power, all of which have their place but which are probably incapable, until efficient energy generation by nuclear fusion is developed, of making the scale of impact required.

The development of animals proceeded from the earliest eukaryotes somewhere from one and a half to two billion years ago along the Darwinian tree of life, although the exact sequence of this is still not completely known. Four hundred million years ago the first vertebrates developed. This is the phylum to which mammals, birds, reptiles, fish and amphibia all belong. A number of these early vertebrates have survived to the present day. Prominent among these are the sharks which have existed in apparently not hugely altered form for about four hundred million years. Humans, by contrast, had their last common ancestor with chimpanzees about six million years ago and our species, Homo sapiens, has existed for less than about five per cent of that time – or some 250,000 years according to recent estimates. If the universe's evolution occurred in just one year it would look like this:

The universe is c.15 billion years old	*(1 year)*
The Earth is c.5 billion years old	*(4 months)*
Earliest life – Archaea – arose c.3–3.5 billion years ago	*(11 weeks)*
First vertebrates c.400–500 million years BP	*(11 days)*

8

First mammals *c.*250 million years BP   *(6 days)*

First primates *c.*55 million years BP   *(32 hours)*

First monkeys *c.*30–35 million years BP   *(19 hours)*

Last shared ancestor of man and   *(3.5 hours)*
chimps *c.*6 million years BP

Origin of Homo sapiens *c.*250,000   *(9 minutes)*
years BP

The agricultural revolution occurred   *(21 seconds)*
*c.*10,000 years BP

Additionally, man has an exceptionally long generation time and there are on average only about three human generations per century. For example, the succession line of the British monarchy from Alfred the Great (born in 849) to Prince George of Cambridge (born in 2013) comprises 37 generations over 1,164 years, giving an average generation time of 31.46 years. Since this is biased to first children and a privileged existence it is likely to be below the overall average. In the past, high infant and childhood mortality were largely responsible for the long generation time. In the very recent past the coming of efficient contraception has allowed childbirth to be delayed by choice. There have therefore been only around 7,000 to 8,000 generations of modern humans. It is worth comparing this with the bacterium *E.Coli* which goes through 8,000 generations in around four months, and with mice which do so in around 1,300 years. In neither of these cases have major evolutionary changes occurred over these time spans.

The study of evolution, certainly from the time of Darwin's grandfather Erasmus Darwin and Jean-Baptiste

Lamarck, Charles Darwin himself and Alfred Wallace and beyond, concentrated largely on the physical remains, the fossils, of earlier life forms. Geological research had already shown that areas that were once under the sea could now be found on mountain tops and had recorded the enormous influence of volcanic activity and earthquakes on the physical environment. The fossil record enabled a fairly convincing tree of life to be built, demonstrating how the various phyla, genera and classes of living organisms may have evolved. This form of study goes on until this day and palaeontological evolutionary biologists often regard themselves as the custodians of Darwinian evolution.

Natural selection drives the evolution of life

The idea that the variety of life forms on Earth are derived from each other, or from earlier forms, goes back to the ancient Greeks, and certainly Socrates believed that most life forms were derived by a form of de-evolution from the human body. Earlier philosophers, for example Anaximander around 600 BC, had speculated that it might be the other way around. However, the biblical account of Genesis, as well as comparable accounts in other major religions, made these speculations unfashionable, certainly in the Western world, for many centuries and it is only with the coming of the European Enlightenment that modern considerations of evolution came to the fore again.

The earliest comprehensive theory of evolution is attributed to Jean-Baptiste Lamarck in 1809. His theory involved the inheritance of acquired characteristics.

The best-known example is that of the giraffe stretching its neck to reach higher forage and passing the longer neck onto its progeny. This caused his theory to be abandoned when August Weismann showed that cutting the tails off mice for several generations did not cause their progeny to have no – or even shorter – tails. (see Tollefsbol, Trygve (2017)

Erasmus Darwin put forward a more modern theory of evolution, though it was not based on experimental data. The great breakthrough was made when Charles Darwin, during the voyage of the *Beagle* when he was accompanying Captain Robert FitzRoy on a mission to map the sea coasts of the world, took the opportunity to make extensive natural history observations. His great idea was that evolution worked by natural selection: those variants which were most successful in a particular environment left the most offspring that would themselves thrive and breed. This theory was published in Darwin's *The Origin of Species by Means of Natural Selection* in 1873. Alfred Russell Wallace had come up with a very similar theory which he sent to Darwin before Darwin first published his own work. Their ideas were presented to a single meeting of The Linnean Society of London on 1 July 1858 by Joseph Hooker and Charles Lyell as neither author could be present.

However, modern understanding of evolution did require information from other sources. The first was the understanding of mechanisms of inheritance. The real pioneer of this was Gregor Mendel and his work on the inheritance of characteristics by peas. His great insight was that these characteristics did not blend but were distinct and were inherited as individual traits. Mendelian genetics defined some characteristics as dominant and others as recessive and showed that they are inherited in a way that depends on having two chromosomes, one derived from the 'father' (the pollen grain) and one derived from the 'mother' (the ovum). This was an outstanding advance. A second outstanding advance came from August Weismann who discovered the separation of germ cells from the soma and showed that inheritance works only through the germ cells with no flow back of characteristics from the soma to the germ cells. On the basis of these discoveries, modern genetic evolutionary mechanisms were defined. In general they have proved very robust.

Further properties of natural selection

Natural selection favours the survival of those who leave the most progeny *that will themselves reproduce*. It is therefore an error to believe that natural selection acts solely during the reproductive period of life. There is an obvious benefit in parents, and particularly the mother, living long enough after the birth of the last offspring for this offspring to achieve sexual maturity and social and economic independence. In humans this period is unusually long and lasts up to a quarter of the anticipated life span.

Another essential feature of natural selection is that it responds to selective pressures operating at that time. It does not, and cannot, anticipate selective pressures that will act in the future; and, even more importantly, it has no goal in view. That is what differentiates natural selection from the artificial selection practised by plant and animal breeders who have definite goals in view. The idea that evolution is a purposive process leading inexorably from earliest life to man was what led Lamarck astray.

Lamarck had also proposed that characteristics acquired in one generation could be passed on to the next. From his studies of individual species in isolated places, Darwin demonstrated that such 'inheritance of acquired characteristics' was unlikely though he did not reject it. His own theories about the communication between soma and germ line, based on the idea of 'pangenesis' and 'gemules', were not experiment-based, were wrong, and were rapidly superseded as knowledge of genetics grew. Evolutionary changes occur not as adaptations but as largely random events which are then selected because they confer survival advantage. An important additional hypothesis – that there is a separation between the soma that interacts with the environment and the germ line that passes genetic information on to the offspring – was put forward by August Weismann in 1893 and this excludes totally any inheritance of acquired characteristics.

By establishing that evolutionary change occurs by natural selection Darwin initiated a fundamentally new approach to the whole of biology. Nevertheless, this new view of evolution preceded any real knowledge of (even) classical genetics let alone molecular genetics and DNA. The Moravian monk Gregor Mendel first described in 1865 his classical three laws of inheritance – segregation, independent assortment and dominance

– based on studies of peas. Darwin may or may not have been aware of Mendel's original work but if he was he did not appreciate its importance.

Social Darwinism and 'the survival of the fittest'

Herbert Spencer was a contemporary of Darwin's and a philosopher and also wrote about evolution. He introduced the phrase 'survival of the fittest' in 1864 in his *Principles of Biology* writing, 'this survival of the fittest which I here sought to express in mechanical terms is that which Mr. Darwin has called natural selection, or the preservation of favoured races in discoverable life'. Spencer was a sociologist as well as a philosopher and applied his evolutionary views to human sociology. It is probably for this reason that the term 'survival of the fittest' acquired unfortunate connotations with the belief that natural selection always involves conflict between competing groups and that it can be regarded as a 'duty' of the fitter groups to eradicate those less fit. This is not inherent in the theory of natural selection and is probably less common than is often believed in animal evolution. A recent example that both Dawkins and David Sloan Wilson quoted, in 2012 and 2015 respectively, is the introduction of the American grey squirrel into the United Kingdom which has caused a great decline in numbers of the native red squirrel, which is a different species. It had long been believed, not only by Dawkins and Wilson, that the loss of red squirrels in areas where grey squirrels had settled was due either to conflict or to direct competition for food. However, neither turned out to be the case. Sainsbury and colleagues demonstrated in 2008 that it is the squirrel pox virus which seems to be the basis of the loss of red squirrels. This virus infects both species of squirrel but, while grey squirrels recover and carry the virus, red squirrels tend to die from this infection. Grey squirrels probably leave the virus in their drays and in the environment in which they feed, and this allows it to pass to the red squirrels who then succumb to it.

It is, however, in relation to human evolution and particularly to competition between human populations that the concept of 'survival of the fittest' – in this connection often referred to as 'Social Darwinism' – has given rise to the most severe problems. It lies at the core of the deep misunderstanding of natural selection by politicians ranging from Karl Marx to Adolf Hitler, who believed that it was in accord with scientific Darwinian principles that superior groups based on class in the case of Marx, and on 'race' in the case of Hitler, should regard it as appropriate, and indeed their duty, to exterminate inferior rivals. This is a total – and a totalitarian – perversion of natural selection and a sad demonstration of how a misunderstood scientific theory in malevolent hands can contribute to appalling social consequences.

The perfection of the human body – the Panglossian delusion

Dr Pangloss, the philosopher in Voltaire's *Candide*, believed that he lived in the best of all possible worlds and it takes a lengthy series of calamities to persuade him otherwise. There is a highly analogous view concerning the perfection of the human body which goes back certainly to the time of the ancient Greeks.

As already mentioned, Socrates was so persuaded of the perfection of (particularly the male) human body that he regarded all other forms of life as deriving from this by a process of reverse evolution (reviewed in Sedley 2007). This idea that the human body is perfect was taken up by the Abrahamic religions – Judaism, Christianity and Islam in chronological order – which held the view that man is created in the image of God, and since God was clearly perfect then man must approach perfection as well. This view has proved extraordinarily durable and was, indeed, adopted by the 19th-century evolutionary thinkers who wished to replace the perfect divine creation with the perfect evolutionary adaptation.

Richard Dawkins, in two of his books, *The Extended Phenotype* (1982) and *The God Delusion* (2006), quotes Richard Lewontin as saying 'that is the one point which I think all evolutionists are agreed upon, that it is virtually impossible to do a better job than an organism is doing in its own environment'. This statement was taken from an oral comment made in a different context during discussion at a meeting in 1967 and Professor Lewontin (personal communication) has said it does not reflect his views. There are many other evolutionary biologists who would also strongly dissent. Students of molecular evolution recognise that evolution, rather than achieving perfection, 'muddles through' and does the best it can. 'Just good enough' is a sufficient criterion for natural selection to be effective.

This is particularly obvious when considering the evolution of humans. The idea that the human body is perfectly designed or engineered does not stand up to even the most superficial examination. The basic skeletal structure seen in man is common to all mammals and evolved for animals that move on all four limbs, rather than for humans who have in fairly recent times adopted an erect posture. Humans are left with bones and, particularly, joints that more often than not wear out within the normal human life span. The number of hip and knee replacements and operations to repair prolapsed intervertebral discs can be seen as a measure of this problem. Since these problems tend to affect mainly the elderly who are beyond their reproductive life, some may believe that they play no great part in natural selection. This is, however, not a convincing argument and the value of 'the grandmother effect' will be discussed later.

Maternal mortality

There is, however, another imperfection in the human body that has been of even greater importance. This is the difficulty, pain and danger that women, when compared with many other mammals, have in giving birth. Karen Rosenberg described in 1992 how this is a further consequence of the upright posture, which has led to constraints on the size and shape of the pelvis which has not allowed the birth canal to expand – particularly to accommodate the increase in size of the human skull needed to accommodate the larger human brain that has accompanied the evolution of Homo sapiens compared with earlier hominid species. That this has turned the apparently pleasurable experience of giving birth in, say, the domestic cat, to the painful and frequently locally damaging experience of human childbirth is sufficient evidence that the human body is very far from perfect. However, the even greater consequence of difficult human childbirth was the high incidence of maternal mortality. Loudon (1992) estimated that in England and Wales there was a death rate of 1,000/100,000 or one per cent of births before 1850. If a woman had (say) 10 pregnancies in her reproductive life this could mean that 10 per cent of women who survived till puberty would die in childbirth. This figure is almost certainly inaccurate as not all pregnancies carry equal risk, but the figure is certainly very considerable and would explain why successful moral communities would not allow their women to engage in warfare or other dangerous activities. It is interesting that in Norse religion Valhalla was reserved for men who died in battle and women who died in childbirth.

In England and Wales maternal mortality had fallen to around 400/100,000 by 1880 and if fell strikingly again after the 1930s. The advent of modern obstetrics, improved contraception and antenatal care, as well as antibiotics, share the credit for greatly reducing maternal mortality. This is one of the great triumphs of modern medicine and has played a greater part in changing the lives of women than is often recognised. In the developed world, the consequent rise in the birth rate has been counteracted by the introduction of effective contraception giving rise to substantial reduction in the average number of children born to a woman. Interestingly, this is no less the case in predominantly Roman Catholic countries in Europe, some of which – Ireland, Italy and Spain – have particularly low birth rates. However, in parts of the developing world these medical advances have been accompanied by a great increase in the number of surviving children and this has fuelled much of the alarming and unsustainable increase in the world population. In other parts of the developing world, notably sub-Saharan Africa, maternal mortality still needs substantial reduction.

The time has surely come when reproduction should be regarded as a privilege rather than a duty and inducements offered to keep family size at a level that will not expand the population. There has been some progress along these lines since the Inter-Academy Panel published its study on population (Royal Society 1994) and it does seem to be the case that providing bathrooms and privacy for women plays an important role in promoting the use of effective contraception.

The human body, therefore, is a good example of the compromises involved in evolutionary adaptation. It is clearly an advantage to have an upright posture and free hands that are available for fine work at all times; but against this has to be balanced the fact that the mechanics of the upright human body are very sub-optimal and do give rise to a great deal of trouble, most particularly for women. Similar trade-offs can be seen in looking at biochemical functions. For example, genetic polymorphisms in complement (a part of the immune system) give rise to the hyperinflammatory complement phenotype. This has been selected in evolution because it gives increased resistance to infection in childhood. However, in later life, this phenotype predisposes to the inflammatory diseases of old age, such as age-related macular degeneration and possibly even atherosclerosis (Lachmann 2009).

The conflict on the level at which natural selection operates – the group, the individual organism or the gene, or any combination of these

This controversy was brought to the attention of the general scientific public in 1976 with the publication of Richard Dawkins's first book *The Selfish Gene*, an account, written for a general audience, of views on evolution put forward initially by the American biologist George Williams in his 1966 book *Adaptation in Natural Selection*. Williams had firmly rejected the seemingly obvious view that natural selection operates at the level of populations of animals – which is known as 'group selection'. Instead he proposed that selection works at the level of individual genes. In 1975, in his book *Sociobiology: The New Synthesis*, Edward Wilson extended the rejection of group selection to the evolution of behaviour and to what is essentially 'cultural' as opposed to 'genetic' evolution. A long-standing diffi-culty for the rejection of group selection was to explain altruism, which can be observed not only in man but in apes and monkeys and, more controversially, in bees as well. William Hamilton (Richard Dawkins's mentor) and others suggested that 'kin selection' could provide an explanation for altruism not requiring group selection. The idea behind the concept of kin selection is that animals can recognise their degree of genetic relationship to others and will behave altruistically to those most closely related to them. They suggested therefore that close genetic similarity lay at the core of altruism. This was based in no small part on considerations of the behaviour of bees, and my clear conclusion as a beekeeper, in contrast to that of Dawkins, is that bees do not recognise genetic relationships at all!

The controversy about the level of selection was not resolved in the 1970s. In 2007, Edward Wilson, the distinguished zoologist who had earlier been an advocate of kin selection, together with D.S. Wilson who had not, together wrote an influential paper – 'Rethinking the theoretical foundation of sociobiology' in favour of multi-level selection. In 2012, Edward Wilson published a book *The Social Conquest of the Earth* to which Richard Dawkins took strong exception. He responded with an article in *Prospect Magazine* called 'The descent of Edward Wilson' which was written in highly aggressive terms. Edward Wilson responded in kind, describing Richard Dawkins as a journalist rather than a scientist, which was reported by Chris Johnston in The Guardian in 2014. D.S. Wilson, in an online article for the Evolution Institute in 2015, analysed the whole controversy and came down firmly in favour of multi-level selection. Without wishing to get involved in this particular controversy as far as genetic evolution is concerned, though I must say I find D.S. Wilson's analysis compelling, I have no doubt whatever that cultural evolution does not work exclusively at the level of the 'meme' (a term introduced by Dawkins as the homologue of the gene in cultural evolution) but works predominantly at group level. Since cultural evolution depends essentially on language and on methods of communication, it is quite difficult to see how one can imagine this could work at the level of any single characteristic. The whole topic of cultural evolution within the human species will be discussed further below.

Mark Cowan, in the online discussion of the *Prospect* article, writes, 'Dawkins and Wilson have something in common, they are both authors in two of the 10+ schools of thought that have tried to generate a theory of culture from evolutionary theory over the last 153 years since "Origin". The reason for that is simple, evolutionary theory cannot [do so].'

Here I attempt to show that, in this matter, Mark Cowan is wrong.

The 1970s controversies provoked me into taking a broader interest in the evolution of behaviour, looking particularly at behavioural differences which distinguish different human populations or 'moral communities', a term admirably defined by Anthony Kenny in 2013. This is a substantially different problem from looking at the behavioural characteristics that distinguish humans from other species – usually their closest relatives, the chimpanzees and bonobos. This is a topic much debated by primatologists (for example by Frans de Waal in 2013) and these differences are clearly genetic.

The differences in behaviour between different human moral communities have developed over a very short time span in evolutionary terms. Our own present species of man, Homo sapiens – sometimes still known as Cro Magnon man – evolved in Southern Africa in the region around 150,000 years ago (Stringer 2011) though recent evidence has pushed this figure back to possibly 250,000 years (Stringer 2016); man and his closest ape relatives last had a common ancestor six million years ago. Bearing in mind that vertebrates originated some four hundred million years ago humans have existed for only 1/1600th of that time.

Genetic Evolution – from Palaeontology

There are two populations of scientists who study genetic evolution. On the one hand, there are those whose principal scientific backgrounds are in natural history and palaeontology and who are in the direct line of succession of Darwin. On the other, there are those whose primary scientific background is in molecular biology and genetics and whose approach is of a very different kind. The two groups are still strangely out of communication.

Darwin was concerned with the origin of separate species and his account of evolution describes the processes by which all different life forms have developed from their earliest common ancestor. Genetic evolution, therefore, covers a period from when the earliest known life forms, the cyanobacteria and Archaea, were known to exist. These primitive organisms were responsible for producing the first free oxygen in the Earth's atmosphere, an absolute prerequisite for the development of animal life. The sequence of evolutionary events studied by palaeontology (the study of the fossil record) and the descriptive account of evolution were highly productive and still occupy the larger part of evolutionary discussion, particularly in the more popular accounts.

The mechanism by which evolutionary change is brought about, however, depends on the study of genetics, and particularly molecular genetics, a discipline which began only with the discovery of the structure of DNA and its method of replication; with the ability to sequence DNA and therefore to study the genome in increasing detail; and with the development of the tools of genetic engineering which allow genes to be inserted or deleted at will. The study of molecular evolution gives a rather different perspective on the mechanisms involved from that given by the fossil approach, which has tended to give the impression that evolution produces perfect adaptations to particular environments.

Molecular Evolution

It was pointed out by Susumo Ohno in his seminal book "Evolution by Gene Duplication" in 1970 that if one has a gene that codes for a protein of importance, it cannot be turned into something else by transcription errors, and that in order to produce new functions, or to provide better control of existing functions, one needs to have currently unused genetic material. This is provided by gene duplication – sometimes by individual genes and sometimes by large regions of chromosomes, sometimes of whole chromosomes and sometimes of the whole genome. These 'pseudogenes' can therefore be regarded both as genes that have died and as genes waiting to be reborn. The recognition that our genome is very much larger than just the genes that are transcribed to give RNA and then protein came with the development of molecular biology, and its significance was not appreciated by the palaeontology-based students of evolution, certainly before the publication of Ohno's book.

It is also really not the case that all mutation is random, if by random we mean that when and where it occurs is equal all over the genome. This is particularly clear to immunologists because the immune system, very unusually, evolves itself substantially in every individual who begins with a limited number of germ-line antibody and T-cell receptor genes and produces a wide variety of these by genetic mechanisms operating in a single life span. It is known from the elegant work of Michael Neuberger, Karuna Ganesh and others on the enzyme adenine inosine deamidase that this produces wide-spread mutation at particular loci by a particular biochemical process. It is also known that rather similar mechanisms occur in viruses where the enzyme is known as Apobec.

The idea that genomic complexity is a sign of intelligent design is therefore perverse. Complexity is a side effect of evolution and not a sign of design, intelligent or otherwise. It also needs to be recognised that genetic evolution uses distinct 'building blocks'. These are the 'protein domains' – independently folding structural units that occur in many different proteins and do not always serve the same function. This was first described by D.B. Wetlaufer in 1973. Protein domains are very long-lived on an evolutionary timescale and only seven per cent of the approximately 1,500 domains known by 2001 were restricted to vertebrates, all the others occurring in invertebrates as well and therefore likely to have originated more than five hundred million years ago.

An analogy can be drawn between molecular evolution and writing computer software. In both cases new products are constructed by selecting from an array of domains or software modules which are put together and then tested for utility. If the product serves its function just well enough it is selected by 'natural selection' and persists. If it does not, it is discarded or may persist as 'junk'. Sydney Brenner frequently (see for example Brenner 2017) distinguished junk – things of no current utility which may be wanted again in the future and are therefore kept – from garbage which has no future utility and is thrown away. However, some 10 per cent of the human genome is taken up by retroviral sequences – traces of long-ago infections with these viruses which have not been removed, although they are probably garbage.

Furthermore, this field still has to take account of the new and growing science of epigenetics, which are inheritable characteristics that are not related directly to DNA sequence but depend on such secondary mechanisms as DNA methylation or histone modification. These are responsible for controlling the pattern of gene expression in different cells and tissues. Furthermore, it has become apparent that RNA itself has major effects on gene transcription and translation. This forms part of the new understanding of 'soft inheritance' (as reviewed by E.J. Richards in 2006) and is also giving rise to novel opportunities for treating disease by inhibiting the expression of particular proteins using inhibitory RNAs. The impact of epigenetics on how we think about molecular evolution is a field that is still developing. The molecular basis of genetic evolution is not at all simple!

The molecular biological revolution began with the observation in 1928 by the British bacteriologist Fred Griffith that injecting mice with a mixture of heat-killed, virulent pneumococci and living, non-virulent pneumococci killed the mice, from which virulent living organisms could then be recovered. This first observation of genetic modification – the gene for virulence having been picked up by the living bacteria from the dead bacteria – was a *discovery* not an *invention*. It is a natural process that bacteria use all the time. Oswald Avery and his colleagues in New York showed in 1944 – to everyone's great surprise – that it was DNA that was responsible for producing this transformation, thereby showing that DNA was the genetic material. As an interesting aside, Fred Griffith was never elected to the Royal Society and was killed in an air raid in 1941, and Oswald Avery and his colleagues were never given a Nobel Prize. The real founders of molecular biology did not receive the recognition that so many of their successors have!

It was the elucidation of the double helix structure of DNA by James Watson and Francis Crick in 1953 that made obvious the mechanism by which genetic inheritance by DNA worked. This gave rise to the enormous advances in molecular biology which have followed since. The understanding of genetic evolution has proved very robust, although its details continue to provide occasional surprises. It is, however, perfectly clear that genetic evolution occurs only at reproduction and that when one is talking of the human species, with its very long reproductive interval, that genetic evolution works very slowly.

Cultural Evolution

It is, however, an entirely different mechanism that accounts for the evolution of differences between distinct human 'moral communities'. This can readily be shown not to be genetic, not only because it happens far too rapidly, but because if children are moved from a primitive culture to an advanced culture they do not retain the characteristics of their birth and adapt to those of their adoptive home. This stands in stark contrast to the analogous situation in the honey bee – a species much favoured by some evolutionary biologists such as Richard Dawkins – in which the exact opposite is the case. The difference in behaviour between different colonies of bees can readily be shown to be entirely genetic. When a colony is re-queened the new workers acquire the characteristics due to their inheritance and learn nothing from the characteristics of the workers they grow up among. All this will be discussed in detail later.

The mechanism by which evolution by natural selection can work on human moral communities is what is known as cultural evolution. Cultural evolution is defined as transmission of characteristics – particularly relating to behaviour, both horizontally and vertically – between generations by any methods other than the involvement of genes. Cultural evolution has been of enormous importance for humans, particularly since the invention of writing about 5,000 years ago. It is, however, extraordinary that cultural evolution has allowed modern humans to progress from the Stone Age to the modern world as we know it in so few generations. This is one of the major topics to be explored – how cultural evolution is brought about in humans and the role that religion plays in this.

Cultural evolution was described in animals by John Tyler Bonner in 1980, and David Attenborough in 1979 described a colony of Japanese macaques on the island of Koshima who learnt to separate rice from sand by throwing the mixture into the sea where the sand sank and the rice floated. However, in any developed form, cultural evolution is uniquely a property of humans and is intimately associated with the development of language. It is language that allows information to be transmitted widely and with far more permanence than is possible by example. Throughout most of human history oral transmission was the mechanism used. About 5,000 years ago, oral transmission was supplemented by the invention of writing. This again allows transmission far more widely and far more permanently; the invention of writing was a hugely important achievement for the human species. About 50 years ago writing began to be supplemented by electronic communication and the effects of this we are only now beginning to see and study.

Cultural evolution, like genetic evolution, is subject to natural selection; those whose behaviour patterns allow them to leave more progeny, who will themselves breed, turn out to be more successful. Again, there is no reason why this competition should involve conflict, although the history of the human species shows that inter-group conflict has been, and remains, extremely common. While cultural evolution does work through natural selection, it is perhaps unwise to draw too close a parallel between the genes of genetic evolution and their equivalent in cultural evolution – memes – the term introduced by Richard Dawkins.

Dawkins coined the term 'meme' as the homologue of the gene and proposed that cultural evolution acts entirely at the level of the meme. This is highly unlikely to be the case. The principal reason for this is that cultural evolution quite clearly acts at the group level, being essentially involved with the development of language and even more so with writing and other forms of communication, which enable information with regard to behaviour and other matters to be transmitted widely and quickly. It is difficult even to draw a model where this would not act on the communicating group rather than any individual, and certainly rather than any meme. The second problem is that the best one can say about the meme is that it is a cute idea to have an analogue of a gene. However, nobody has yet been able to define a meme in any sense that would allow it to be measured or analysed in any objective fashion. The structure of genes is now well known – they can be sequenced, they can be modified, they can be knocked out, they have a real physical existence. None of this is true of memes, nor is there any evidence of transmission of memes that is in any way analogous with the transmission of genes; there is no non-blending inheritance and no obvious dominant or recessive effect. It is fairly clear that cultural evolution does work entirely at the group level and that it primarily enshrines prescriptions both for behaviour in the moral and ethical sense and with regard to the ordinary matters of living, such as diet, clothing, social interaction, sexual behaviour, etc.

Edward Wilson coined the term 'culturegen' as the analogue of the gene in cultural evolution, which he envisaged as acting in conjunction with conventional genetic genes as a selective mechanism. This must be true at certain levels; the example given is that organisms that do not have a larynx suitable for speech cannot learn to talk. However, the reverse is clearly not true since birds can speak perfectly well but have never developed speech except in a fully imitative fashion. For most purposes, the time scales are totally incompatible. Genetic evolution, particularly in species with long generation times, such as humans, is really quite slow, whereas cultural evolution is very rapid. The two, therefore, are very difficult to mesh and are largely, though not entirely, separate.

For this reason alone one can be confident that the development of distinct human moral communities is not the consequence of genetic evolution – changes that affect the genome – but is indeed cultural. While the idea of cultural evolution goes back at least as far as Darwin, ideas on how it is brought about have changed greatly since the mechanisms of genetic evolution have become so much clearer with the advent of molecular biology. In both types of evolution it is necessary that for natural selection to work on a particular trait, this trait must be maintained in a stable way. For genetic evolution, this stability is 'built in' to the DNA. For cultural evolution, on the other hand, there is a need for a mechanism that maintains the stability of a behavioural variant over enough individuals and over a long enough period of time, measured in generations, for natural selection to be able to act upon it. This is where religion comes into the picture. The thesis that is here proposed is that the 'prescriptions' with regard to human behaviour – the 'thou shalts' and the 'thou shalt nots' – that are a constant feature of all religions of which we have sufficient knowledge, have as their essential function the role of providing the stability needed for natural selection to be able to work for cultural evolution. Furthermore, it is proposed that religious prescription is the essential element of religions that accounts for their almost universal occurrence in human society, and that the other major (but more variable) elements that make up religions – God or gods, heaven and/or hell, an afterlife and/or reincarnation – serve principally to enforce the prescription.

Ernest Kellet pointed out in 1933 in his book *A Short History of Religions* that 'in almost all nations, till comparatively recent times, that which all are agreed to call religion had little or nothing to do with morality'. Their prescriptions concentrate on such other matters as, for example, dress and diet. The prescriptions for some major religions (in alphabetical order) are summarised in Tables 1 and 2 .

What is Religion?

An extra-terrestrial anthropologist studying the habits of the human species would be struck by how prominent a part religion has played in human society from the earliest times we know of. Being a thoroughly modern anthropologist, that being might first consult a search engine and find that 'religion' elicits 233 million hits. One of these would direct the anthropologist to Wikipedia and a definition of religion as 'a set of beliefs concerning the cause, nature and purpose of life and the universe, especially when one considers the creation of the supernatural agency or human beings' relation to that which they consider sacred, spiritual and divine'. A probably more satisfactory (to me at any rate) definition of religion was given by Dr Johnson in *A Dictionary of the English Language* over two centuries ago. He defined religion as 'virtue as founded upon reverence of God in expectation of future rewards or punishments'. All definitions, of course, require further definitions of some of the words they contain, including divine, spiritual, supernatural and God. However, there can be no doubt that the topic, however defined, has a very long history and still plays a hugely important role in contemporary human society. This can be seen very simply in terms of the number and extent of the religious buildings that can be found throughout the world, the number of people employed by or for religions, and the intense controversy that the whole subject evokes today.

The archaeological and historical background

As far as we know, modern humans, Homo sapiens, arose in Africa probably around 250,000 years ago and spread from there originally along the coasts of the Arabian Peninsula towards Asia. They had colonised much of the Eurasian and Australasian land mass by about 75,000 years ago, and the Americas somewhat more recently – about 25,000 years ago. However, these figures are all subject to revision as further archaeological discoveries are made.

Of the first 200,000 years or so of human existence we know only from archaeological evidence, since there are no other records of what these early humans thought or believed or how they organised their societies. The view of early religion is derived from observations on burial customs. The practice of burying bodies oriented in particular directions with grave goods and other artefacts inside their graves can be regarded as an epiphenomenon of religion. If this is the case then the oldest religious artefacts so far found are from about 70,000 years ago in a cave in Botswana, as documented by Sheila Coulson in 2006.

It has been very plausibly argued by Ara Norenzayan (2013) that 'pro-social' religions arose to meet the needs of larger communities to co-operate, following the agricultural revolution about 10,000 years ago, and that these religions developed 'Big Gods'. Others have argued that it was humans' recognition of their mortality from an early age that gave rise to the consoling belief in some form of continued existence after death. This belief is a feature of the Abrahamic religions and may be much, much older. However, not all religions have either Big Gods (or indeed any gods) or belief in continued existence after death. What all religions that we know enough about do share is a 'prescription' – they lay down commandments and prohibitions on how their adherents should behave. The central argument to be put forward here is that it is religious prescription that has given religions their enduring importance in human society, that these prescriptions allow particular patterns of behaviour to be maintained in a stable form over many generations in different human religious communities, and that this allows natural selection to act upon these behaviours and thereby allows the cultural (rather than genetic) evolution of important aspects of human behaviour.

Charles Darwin himself was well aware that his theory of evolution by natural selection contradicted the Genesis account of creation. The religious establishment of the time opposed the whole idea of evolution – particularly where evolution of the human species was concerned – and has continued to do so in varying degrees ever since. However, Darwin was buried in Westminster Abbey, reflecting his acceptance by the British establishment by the time of his death. Thomas Huxley, Charles Darwin's principal contemporary advocate, accepted evolution entirely but took the view that morality – which he viewed as being derived from religion – was there to counteract the 'cosmic struggle for existence', which was how he regarded evolution by natural selection. His views are discussed further below.

I will argue that Huxley's concern was mistaken and that, far from religion standing in opposition to evolution by natural selection, religions supply the building blocks which allow 'cultural' as opposed to 'genetic' evolution in humans to function.

By contrast, in recent years the 'neo-atheists' – Victor Stenger, Christopher Hitchins and Richard Dawkins

– have pointed out that throughout historical times the effects of religion appear to have been overwhelmingly harmful. This is in large part due to the extreme intolerance of one religion for another and the interminable warfare and oppression to which this has given rise. They seem to regard religion as some form of pathological process built into the human psyche. That hypothesis, however, is hardly appealing to any student of evolution. If religion of one sort or another has persisted for as long as archaeological evidence would suggest, then it has been with us for most of the known existence of Homo sapiens, which would again suggest extremely strongly that there must be some valuable function to religion that balances the harmful effects laid out by the neo-atheists.

The question that I therefore want to address is why religions of one kind or another should have survived so successfully over very long periods of human evolutionary time, notwithstanding the fact that they clearly have given rise to much conflict and suffering. In principle, this question can be asked without reference to any currently existing religions, none of which is more than about 5,000 years old. It is possible that shamanistic religions – some of which still survive – may be older but they do not have holy books to inform us. The contenders for the oldest religions still being practised are Zoroastrianism and Judaism, which both originate somewhere around 5,000 BP. Although there is good archaeological evidence that there were much older religions, in the absence of written records we do not know in any detail the nature of their teachings which makes discussion of religions with an historical record inevitable.

The oldest religions of which we have knowledge were shamanistic. The word 'shaman' means 'one who knows' and shamans were common in Northern Asia, in the Arctic regions and in many other hunter-gatherer cultures. The shaman was believed to be able to communicate with the spirit world and bring both benefit and harm to his or her community. Although important in regard to birth, marriage and death, and also involved in sickness and its cure, it is not immediately clear what made up the prescriptive element of shamanistic religions but there seems little doubt that they were concerned with many aspects of group behaviour.

Virtue – Johnson's first component of religion

The prescriptive elements in most religions deal with similar aspects of human behaviour. These include diet and health, reproductive behaviour, interpersonal relationships (particularly honesty and truthfulness), attitudes to work and attitudes to death and suicide. It is unfortunately the case that information about the prescriptions of religions that died out long ago are usually unknown to us because they were not written down, and even where written accounts exist they are usually devoted to describing rituals rather than prescriptions. However, as far as is known, religious prescriptions turn out to encourage behaviours that lead to an increase in population. The ethical paradigm of all religions we know about is really that of an endangered species in which the primary obligation of the male is to feed and defend his mate and his children and the primary obligation of the female is to bear children However, this should not be taken to mean that particular elements of religious prescription were designed with population increase in mind. It is extremely unlikely that any prophet ever went into the wilderness to contemplate what forms of behaviour would cause their believers to produce more progeny. The origin of behavioural precepts in most cases is almost certainly entirely unrelated to their evolutionary selective advantage. A good example is the practice of male circumcision. Those introducing this practice will not have had in mind its beneficial effect on the spread of sexually transmitted diseases. It is, however, highly plausible that the reduction in the spread of human papilloma viruses (an important cause of cancer of the cervix in women and some other tumours in men), and much more recently of HIV, explain why the practice was of selective advantage. Karl Popper's view on the origin of scientific hypotheses (Popper 1934), that innovations are random, aesthetic or inspirational, is likely to be equally applicable to innovations in behavioural prescriptions. It has often been suggested that modern capitalist society arose as a consequence of behavioural changes introduced by the Reformation associated with Protestant teachings on honesty in trading.

This view of religious virtue as providing the building blocks of human cultural evolution carries with it the conclusions that humans do have a degree of free will and that ethical standards (which are the formulation by which religious prescriptions are recognised as being good rather than bad) are not permanently fixed and do themselves evolve. It is curious that this conclusion was not adopted by the 19th-century evolutionary scientists. Indeed, Thomas Huxley took the opposite view. He regarded ethics as being there to oppose and control the 'cosmic struggle for existence':

'As I have already urged, the practice of that which is ethically best – what we call goodness or virtue – involves a course of conduct which in all respects, is opposed to that which leads to success in the cosmic struggle for existence. In place of ruthless self-assertion it demands self-restraint; in place of thrusting aside, or treading down, all competitors, it requires that the individual shall not merely respect, but shall help his fellows; its influence is directed, not so much to the survival of the fittest, as to the fitting of as many as possible to survive.

'Laws and moral precepts are directed to the end of curbing the cosmic process and reminding the individual of his duty to the community, to the protection and influence of which he owes, if not existence itself, at least the life of something better than a brutal savage.

'The struggle for existence which has done such admirable work in cosmic nature, must, it appears, be equally beneficent in the ethical sphere. Yet if that which I have insisted upon is true; if the cosmic process has no sort of relation to moral ends; if the imitation of it by man is inconsistent with the first principles of ethics; what becomes of this surprising theory?

'Let us understand, once for all, that the ethical progress of society depends, not on imitating the cosmic process, still less in running away from it, but in combating it.'

Natural Law and the Evolution of Ethics

This idea that ethics are a permanent and unchangeable feature of human society is not confined to Thomas Huxley. It is still held by those who believe in 'natural law' – that there is a fixed ethical paradigm that derives from God. Natural law is a very long-standing philosophical theory which was derived originally from the Stoics and then via Aristotle and Saint Thomas Aquinas, who wrote 'there must be something which is to all beings the cause of there being goodness and every other perfection, and this we call God' into current religious philosophy, particularly among Roman Catholics. Although inevitably a philosophical theory of this age and complexity is not easily epitomised briefly, it has been described by Jonathon Dolhenty (2012) as sharing the following characteristics:

'Natural law is not made by human beings,
is based on the structure of reality itself,
is the same for all human beings and at all times,
is an unchanging rule or pattern which is there for human beings to discover,
is the naturally knowable moral law,
is a means by which human beings can rationally guide themselves to the good.'

This concept of an unchanging ethical structure, which is the same for all human beings and at all times, is incompatible with religious and ethical prescription acting as the building blocks of cultural evolution. It is also, even on cursory inspection, unlikely to be true.

There are certainly a number of moral precepts or ethical prescriptions that seem not to vary among different religious prescriptions and seem to have been maintained by virtually all the cultures of which we know. These include altruism, respect for human life and dignity, truthfulness and honesty. One can conclude that these are more or less necessary for the long-term survival of human society and form the core of contemporary and 'universal' ethical prescription.

However, cultures have held widely different ethical views on a number of other issues of which human sacrifice, cannibalism, slavery and suicide are just four examples. The belief in natural law, therefore, would carry with it the view that many of the ancestor civilisations we hold in high regard, such as the ancient Greeks, who were apparently comfortable with slavery, or the high civilisations of the Americas which had an inordinate capacity for human sacrifice and believed this to be a requirement for the continuation of life, were grossly morally defective. This is a conclusion which one might not wish to defend.

Can one now see on looking back any justification for why these practices, which contemporary ethical culture has largely rejected, might have had a selective advantage in the past?

Slavery is a particularly challenging example. It is conceivable that in very ancient warfare it may have proved advantageous for the winners to kill the men they had defeated and take the women as slaves. This can still be recognised in the story of the rape of the Sabine women in the early history of Rome. Taking captive women as slaves may be the oldest form of slavery and may well have carried a selective advantage in the enlargement of the gene pool which would result from interbreeding with a separate population. In the rather small population pools that will have existed in Neolithic times this may have led to selective success, particularly in resisting contagious disease, by bringing in a larger variety of variants in the genes involved in immunity. Since human populations have grown and found other ways of expanding the gene pool with which they breed, the other features of slavery – its injustice and inhumanity and its complete incompatibility with the basic ethical principle that all humans are equal morally and before the law – should have caused its total and universal ethical rejection. This was, however, not at all the case and very widespread slavery has existed in most human cultures throughout recorded history. It is really only with the coming of the European Enlightenment that the rejection of slavery was promoted with vigour, and it was not until the 19th century that slavery was finally abolished in the United States. This demonstrates that the evolution of ethics does not always run smoothly (as can also be seen in the more recent past).

Cannibalism has been found in modern times only in remote populations and there may be a good reason why the practice of cannibalism died out. This is associated not with the morality of eating the dead but with the transmission of spongiform encephalopathies. These are lethal diseases affecting the brain which are caused by transmissible proteins (prions) that can spread by eating affected tissue – particularly brain. Here we do have the real example of the Fore tribe in New Guinea, which practised a form of ritual cannibalism out of respect for the dead. This gave rise to an epidemic of Kuru, a spongiform encephalopathy that very nearly wiped out the Fore tribe in the first half of the 20th century. Only the prohibition of cannibalism by the Australians, who then governed New Guinea, allowed this population to survive.

Human sacrifice also has an ancient history as can be seen in the story of Abraham being prepared to sacrifice his son Isaac in the Old Testament. It was practised to an extraordinary extent by American cultures, ranging from the Incas and their predecessors to the Aztecs. It is difficult to see now what advantage this might have brought to the populations that practised it. It is conceivable that as a method of population control it avoided depletion of resources in marginal communities. This might be argued along the lines of forms of ritual suicide described among some Pacific islanders by Jared Diamond in his 2005 book *Collapse*. This is unlikely to have been the case in the Americas, where resources seem to have been quite plentiful.

Attitudes to suicide are still variable among contemporary cultures, and the right to die is regarded by many, including me, as a corollary to the right to life. There is no obvious explanation of why the moral rejection of suicide should have adaptive value, though this may well be part of the general moral ethic of an endangered species whose primary concern is to increase its numbers.

Some ethical evolution has been observed in recent times: it has been suggested that it was the Reformation that brought with it the ethical demand that traders should ask only the lowest price that they were willing to accept rather than to rely on bargaining with their customers to produce a sale. If so, this came from views on salvation and was not directly aimed at promoting capitalism. Certainly the Enlightenment brought with it substantial changes in moral philosophy and the justification of the modern moral prescription in terms of reason.

However, it is important to realise that, just as genetic evolution has no goal and evolved innovations are not always successful and may subsequently die out, the same is true of cultural evolution. The long-standing ethical paradigm of most religious prescriptions enshrines the primary priority of an endangered species – to increase numbers. It is presumably this imperative that lay at the core of the success of the prohibitions of forms of sexual activity that do not give rise to children, of the refusal to allow abortions or contraception, and of the imposition as a primary duty on women to bear and bring up children. It is clear enough that human beings are no longer an endangered species. The reverse is now the case, and the uncontrolled growth in the human population brought about by advances in producing food, in public health and in the control of infectious disease, has given rise to the opposite situation where the human population is now recognised as endangering the physical conditions on the planet that are conducive to life. It is, therefore, entirely obvious that a change in all these ethical parameters is urgently needed, but it has proved extremely difficult to bring these about. Some have indeed occurred – the emancipation of women is a clear example of an idea that is by no means new, but is now no longer unadaptive, and therefore those populations which allow women to reject the idea that they need to have children are unlikely to die out. To some extent the same is probably true of the liberalisation of the attitude to homosexual relationships that do not give rise to children. However, the general acceptance of contraception and the right to abortion are still fiercely contested, particularly by the Roman Catholic Church on the grounds that this is contrary to 'natural law'.

Much more disturbingly, the twentieth century showed that there are ways of trying to deal with these problems, but the solution was much worse than the disease. The outstanding example of this, of course, is National Socialism in Germany, which was a secular religion based on a doctrine of racial superiority and the belief that the solution to many of the problems produced by modern advances was to destroy 'inferior races'. This was believed to be a Darwinian solution. As already discussed, this was a gross misunderstanding of Social Darwinism. Nevertheless, the behavioural prescription of the Nazis, which was enforced largely by physical coercion, did achieve for a few years, in Germany, quite astonishing acceptance by the population. Even in the fairly short term this prescription turned out to be highly disadvantageous, as can be seen in the result of World War Two. Nevertheless, the existence of Nazism is deeply disturbing particularly to all those who believe that ethical progress is inevitable – who have a Lamarckian view of cultural evolution rather than the harsher Darwinian view.

World communism enshrined a similar misunderstanding of Darwin, although the Marxian ideal was less vicious than that of the National Socialists. However, in the hands of Stalin or Pol Pot or Mao, the eradication of certain classes was held to be a prerequisite for building the society they felt was ethically desirable.

One must therefore conclude that ethics has evolved and will continue to evolve by natural selection, which carries with it the conclusion already discussed that there is probably neither prospect nor real advantage in trying to secure a single universal ethic on issues that are in any way controversial; the universal ethic will be of a very general kind enshrining those dictates that have been selected over very many cultures for very long periods of time. All others do need to compete so they can be tested by selection to see what is advantageous to the community in which we now live. However, as the human population now fills the planet, the timescales to allow such competition to occur may have to be rather shorter than they have been in the past, and there may have to be more general agreement on such things as controlling climate change or the exhaustion of essential resources which cannot be done just for one population when other larger populations do the reverse. To some extent, therefore, we are in a new environment which will affect the mechanisms by which cultural evolution can produce its results.

The soul

The definition of the term 'soul' is not easy to come by. There is a huge range of definitions certainly going back to the ancient Egyptians and Greeks, and some concept of soul or psyche is to be found in most religions. The ancient Egyptians believed that the soul survived in the afterlife as long as the body was preserved, accounting for all the trouble they took to preserve mummies. Aristotle, sensible as he usually was, taught that the soul was an intrinsic part of the body and did not survive it. The more common religious definition of the soul is that it is independent of the body, and many religions believe that it survives the death of the body and that this non-corporeal part of the human being can either be reincarnated into another human being, or, in some religions, into another animal, or that it is what passes into an afterlife either to enjoy the rewards of virtue or to suffer the punishments of sin.

If one takes this kind of definition it is then reasonable to ask at what stage in human development does the soul 'enter' the body? A rather similar question is asked in secular terms, when it is ethically necessary to decide at what stage of development an embryo or a foetus acquires the status of a human being and requires to be treated as such. The ancient and mediaeval Church originally took its lead on this subject from Aristotle and taught that foetus vegetalis became foetus animalis and then foetus animatus at a time when its gender could be clearly recognised. Curiously this was reckoned to be 40 days for a male and 80 or 90 days for a female. Being rather easier to ascertain, the occurrence of quickening, when the woman first feels the presence of the baby inside her, was held by various religious teachers to be the time when the foetus could be held to be a human being. This is often around 18 to 20 weeks of gestation (or a little earlier in pregnancies after the first). However, not all religions agreed on this. In Judaism, an interpretation of Genesis was that life was breathed by God into the baby when it was born, so that the acquisition of the soul or human dignity did not occur till birth.

In the 19th century, studies of human and animal development established the phenomenon of fertilisation during which the sperm fuses with the egg to give rise to the conceptus. Probably in order to keep Papal teaching in line with what was then contemporary embryology, but possibly also to reduce the numbers of early abortions that were then taking place, Pius IX in 1869 issued the Bull *Apostolicae Sedis* declaring that ensoulment occurred at conception and effectively saying that full human dignity should be accorded to all stages of human deve-lopment from the moment of conception onwards. This remains the teaching of the Catholic Church. Similar views are held by the 'pro-life' lobby of which the Society for the Protection of Unborn Children (SPUC) is a typical member[1]. The action taken by Pius IX, inasmuch as he was trying to keep doctrine in accord with contemporary science, should not simply have been left at this particular moment in the 19th century because the study of embryo-logy continued to progress, and once doctrine is adapted to conform with scientific discovery this adaptation needs to be on a continuous basis in order to keep pace with the progress of the relevant science.

---

[1] Their website gives full details: http://www.spuc.org.uk/

What Pius IX (and everyone else) did not know in 1869 was that the majority of fertilised ova do not even implant in the uterus. Women are not aware of them and they are shed with the menstrual flow. These concepti, to which the Roman Catholic Church affords full human status, are neither recognised nor mourned nor buried. If one accepts the Pius IX point of view, it inevitably follows that the majority population of heaven (for those who subscribe to the idea that the dead go to heaven or hell immediately rather than waiting in limbo until after the Second Coming) will be these undifferentiated single cell concepti that have known no contact with the outside world and which therefore certainly cannot have sinned. It is difficult to believe that this is what Pius IX actually had in mind and it is astonishing that his successors have been prepared to keep what is so clearly an absurd doctrine. This really is fideism taken to an extreme.

Yet further problems for ensoulment at conception have arisen from yet further advances in developmental biology. A fertilised ovum can clearly enjoy no human status on its own account. Those who wish to attribute any form of human status to the fertilised ovum do so on the basis of its potential to acquire such status – as they do also, albeit to a decreasing extent, to later foetuses. However, the proposition that anything with the potential to become an adult human should be accorded full human dignity has been reduced to total absurdity since it has been shown that somatic cells (for example skin fibroblasts) can be de-differentiated in vitro and their nuclei injected into an enucleated ovum to give rise, after implantation into a uterus, to a viable animal – the 'Dolly phenomenon' as shown by

Wilmut and his colleagues in 1997. This would make it necessary, on the basis of their potential, to give all human cells the status of human beings. As one journalist put it, this would lead to our having to 'bury our dandruff'. Those who sought a weasel way out of this difficulty by attaching some unspecified special status to the ovum have also been proved wrong by the more recent work of Kazutoshi Takahashi and Shinya Yanamaka in 2006 showing that adult fibroblasts can be reprogrammed in vitro into pluripotent stem cells which can give rise to embryo formation.

The conclusion therefore is inescapable. It is impossible to define human status solely on the basis of potential and therefore the fundamentalist view that human status should be accorded to the fertilised ovum has to be rejected. The 'slippery slope' argument is frequently used as a fall-back position when all other rational argument has failed. It is, however, intrinsically flawed, as the philosopher Francis Cornford pointed out in a rather different context. He refers to it as 'The Principle of the Wedge':

'The Principle of the Wedge is that you should not act justly now for fear of raising expectations that you may act still more justly in the future – expectations which you are afraid you will not have the courage to satisfy. A little reflection will make it evident that the Wedge argument implies the admission that the persons who use it cannot prove that the action is not just. If they could, that would be the sole and sufficient reason for not doing it and this argument would be superfluous.'

The decision on when to accord any form of human status to a growing embryo has therefore to be made on different and more rational grounds.

One defensible proposition is to hold that before the foetus has developed at least one sense organ it can make no contact of any kind with the outside world and therefore no human status can be accorded it. This would place the initial moment for acquiring any status at the end of the first trimester of pregnancy. As the foetus develops sense organs and a nervous system it gradually acquires human status; fully human status is accorded in most cultures at birth.

Another, and widely used, proposition is to accord substantial human status to the foetus when it is capable of independent life outside the uterus. This is the criterion used in British law. It has the disadvantage that developments in the techniques for keeping very small babies alive have, and may continue, to reduce this critical time. It used to be 28 weeks of gestation and was reduced to 24 weeks in 1990. The follow-up data on very premature babies as reported by Costeloe and colleagues in 2000 and by Larroque and colleagues in 2008 is, however, not encouraging, as a substantial proportion go on to have quite severe problems later on. These conclusions accord quite well with the law in Great Britain where a foetus below 24 weeks of gestation can be aborted for health, economic or social reasons. For later pregnancies, abortion is still allowed but only if there is grave risk to the life of the woman, evidence of severe foetal abnormality or risk of grave physical and mental injury to the woman. A range of analogous regulations are in place in much of Europe though many have gestational time limits of 12 weeks and the conditions that have to be met are also rather variable[2]. Just for once, it is not the law which is the ass.

Religious prescription or virtue in a secular world

Some incorporation of ethical prescription into a system of secular law goes back certainly as far as the code of Hammurabi, from the First Babylonian dynasty about 5,000 years ago. As a consequence of the European Enlightenment in the second half of the 17th and the 18th centuries, moral philosophers codified ethics on a more rational basis although its religious origins were not abandoned. The concept of human rights can be found in mediaeval thought and was extended by the European Enlightenment and can be encapsulated in the preamble to the American Declaration of Independence (1776): 'We hold these truths to be self-evident, that all men are created equal, that they are endowed by their Creator with certain unalienable Rights that among these are Life, Liberty and the pursuit of Happiness', and in Immanuel Kant's injunction that 'humanity is an end in itself' (Kant ,1785). In modern secular societies, separation of Church and State is widespread but patchy and in those Muslim countries that still operate Sharia law the separation is very incomplete. Even in the United Kingdom, questions of conscience when voted

---

[2] For the situation in European countries in 2018 see https://www.france24.com/en/20180525-abortion-laws-vary-eu-ireland-malta-poland-termination

on in the United Kingdom parliament are often left to a free vote, suggesting that MPs should be guided by considerations other than those that they normally consider when making laws.

Rights – even those listed above – are never absolute and all are subject to derogation for good cause. The right to life is always temporary as everyone dies; the right to liberty can be over-ridden by the criminal law; and the pursuit of happiness is limited where it interferes with the happiness of others. Freedom of speech, which is frequently claimed to be (almost) absolute, is limited by libel, by restrictions on hate speech and, in some cultures, by blasphemy. In general, rights can only be claimed while duties can be enforced. A good case can be made that in general there are no rights where there are no duties. Exceptions are made for the very young and the very old where rights derive from future or past duties! However, animals have no duties and there is a good case for denying rights to animals while acknowledging that humans certainly have duties towards animals. As has become increasingly apparent with the dangers of global warming, humans also have duties to plants and to biodiversity although no one claims that plants have rights.

Reverence of God and expectation of future rewards – Johnson's second and third components of religion

Johnson's second component is 'reverence of God', God not being further defined, but being, presumably, a supernatural being (or beings) whose attributes will usually include immortality and both wisdom and power superior to that of human beings.

There are three distinct concepts of God. There is the god who created the universe and manages it (Theism), the god who created the universe but takes no part in managing it (Deism), and the god who neither created nor manages the universe and is purely contemplative and therefore unknowable. The god of Abraham clearly falls into the first group. This is difficult to reconcile with the interminable warfare between different worshippers of this same god who always believe that (s)he is on their side.

Johnson's third component is the 'expectation of future rewards and punishments', which in most traditional religions are rewards and punishments to be expected after death, and therefore presuppose some continuation of existence after physical death either in another world or after reincarnation.

The details of both of these latter components, 'God' and 'afterlife', are extremely variable. Not all religions have both, although most have one or the other.

God(s)

The nature of 'God', or gods, varies greatly among different religions. Early shamanistic religions are believed to have worshipped animals. For example, the carving of a serpent, which was discovered in a cave in the Tsodilo Hills in Botswana, is apparently 70,000 years old and is believed to be the oldest, plausible religious artefact yet discovered. Two pieces of worked ochre in the Blombos cave in South Africa described by Henshilwood and colleagues in 2011 are of similar age and are held to have been used for ritual purposes. Other shamanistic religions also worship rocks and rivers and other natural phenomena. Many more recent religions have been more anthropomorphic in concept with two opposed views of the relationship between mankind and God(s): one is that man was created by and in the image of God; the other is that god(s) were created by, and in the image of, the men that worship them.

The Abrahamic religions believe in a single god – an idea which seems to have originated with Akhenaton in ancient Egypt in the 14th century BC (where it did not long survive him). Zoroastrianism, which competes with Judaism for being the oldest religion still practised today, also has a single god – Ahura Mazda – with a main adversary – Angra Mainyu – and teachings that show significant similarity to those of the Abrahamic religions. Other ancient Egyptian religions and the religions of Classical Greece and Rome were highly polytheistic as were the Nordic religions and as is Hinduism today. Nor were all gods immortal. Roman and various oriental emperors were worshipped as gods in their own lifetimes and the Emperor of Japan was worshipped as a god well into the twentieth century. The Gods of Valhalla were eventually not immortal either.

Demagods

One class of god, for whom I propose to use the name 'demagod' as a deified form of 'demagogue', certainly existed. They were human leaders who put forward their own prescriptions using the power of their oratory and their personality, and enforced them by physical coercion rather than by hope and fears of rewards and punishments in an afterlife. When these demagogues became sufficiently powerful they were accorded many of the attributes of godhood. Although demagods are certainly not new they became a major phenomenon in the 20th century. It is worthwhile to ask whether religion in general has discouraged demagods or has encouraged their emergence. It seems clear that they are not restricted to particular religions. Attila the Hun (433–453 AD) may be one of the earlier figures from ancient times who can be classified as a demagod and his religion was probably shamanistic. Genghis Khan in the 13th century probably qualifies too and followed a similar religion. His distant descendant Timur (Tamerlane – the scourge of God), in the 15th century, certainly qualifies, and he was a Muslim. What is, however, clear is that the modern secular religions have produced demagods with alarming regularity. The fascist leaders were probably all demagods to a varying extent, depending on how much power they exercised.

Hitler was the archetype of the demagod. The practice imposed by the Nazis of giving a salute and saying 'Heil Hitler' as the normal form of greeting replacing the traditional 'Grüss Gott' is a striking manifestation. Hitler may well qualify also as the most damaging demagod ever, but the lesser fascist dictators like Mussolini in Italy and Horthi in Hungary showed similar tendencies. It is even more depressing that communism, which in its original intent was a more admirable creed, has nevertheless produced frequent demagods. Stalin was the outstanding example and Mao Tse Tung in China, Pol Pot in Cambodia and Ceausescu in Romania all qualify.

It is not necessary to expand this list any further. It is amply clear that the secular religions – that came to fill the vacuum left, for many who wished to believe, by the increase in scientific knowledge that undermined their traditional religions – are particularly prone to pandering to the very worst aspects of human nature and they have particularly embraced racism, xenophobia and genocide.

The catastrophic track record of secular religions and of the demagods they have fostered needs always to be borne in mind. Exposing the errors of an existing system does not automatically lead to an improvement in human welfare and has indeed had exactly the opposite effect. There can be no serious doubt that the rational approach to life is correct inasmuch as it is supported by all the empirical evidence we have. This does not mean that it will be easy to persuade the bulk of humanity to accept it as the basis for action. Of course, the traditional religions have been similarly responsible for producing their own demagods, and detailed accounts of this can be found both in Chris Hitchens's *God is not Great* and Richard Dawkins's *The God Delusion*. From the religious wars that afflicted Europe in the Middle Ages to the jihads of the Muslims that are still with us, the major current world religions are no shining example of human kindness or generosity. The genocidal violence that afflicted India immediately after independence and partition is another recent example of religious intolerance taking lethal forms. All who write about religion, not least the sceptics and unbelievers, should bear this appalling saga in mind and remember that pointing out to people the folly of some of what they believe will not necessarily lead, in the short term at least, to a better-behaved world.

To paraphrase Hamlet: It may be better to bear those gods we have than fly to others that we know not of.

Religions Without Gods

Confucianism

One good example of a highly successful religion, subscribing to those characteristics which I have defined as making up a religion, is Confucianism (see Oldstone-Moore 2002). Confucius lived from 551 to 478 BC and developed a system of ethical and socio-political teaching which has had an enduring and important influence on ethical behaviour in China and the Far East. Essentially, Confucianism is a philosophy and system of ethical behaviour which teaches that human beings can become better on the basis of their own endeavours. It emphasises three cardinal virtues: ren, yi and vli, where ren is a declaration of altruism, yi is virtuous morality, and vli is a system of norms of how people should act which can be summed up as 'do as you would be done by'. Confucianism does not require a belief in God or indeed of an afterlife or of the supernatural at all. There is an element of ancestor worship to Confucianism but the term 'worship' here is probably used in a slightly different sense and involves respect for one's ancestors rather than regarding them as having supernatural characteristics. In the Far East, various religions both older and subsequent to Confucianism became somewhat merged so that accounts of quite various kinds can be found.

Buddha and Buddhism

Gautama Sakyamuna was born about 566 BCE, the son of the ruler of a kingdom in north-east India. Distressed by all the unhappiness among the population, he gave up his privileges and left his father's palace seeking a teacher for the right way to live. Originally he joined the Jain sect but found the rigorous discipline made him ill and unable to meditate, so he adopted what he called 'The Middle Way' and concluded that suffering was due to excess desire and could gradually be eliminated. He regarded 'nirvana' as the state to which living beings should finally aspire and as reserved for those who had acquired enlightenment and had rid themselves of all desires. The original form of Buddhism did not have a god and indeed Buddha taught that belief in God was itself a desire which had to be disposed of before one could achieve nirvana. Buddha did believe, as did many at that time, in reincarnation, not necessarily in human form, and it was after a number of lives that one would achieve nirvana and escape from the cycle of birth and rebirth. In some ways the position of Buddha is not dissimilar to that of many secular thinkers of the modern era, except that they believe that nirvana is achieved by everyone at the end of a single life and is achieved without the need to abolish all desires before death.

After his death Buddha's disciples continued to teach 'the Buddhist Way' but his philosophy was not regarded as a religion until the late third century BC. In about 260 BC the Mauryan king Ashoka from the Ganges Plain fought a long and cruel war against the eastern state of Kalinga. Though he won he was terribly shocked by the destruction and bloodshed. He became a pacifist and promoted the concept of Dharma – social and religious principles – by erecting pillars and rock carvings around his extensive empire, each carved in the languages appropriate to the region. As a result Buddhism became elevated to a religion, and subsequently spread though the Indian subcontinent and Asia. In these widely differing settings it was influenced by other local religions, resulting in different schools of Buddhism. Some analogy can be seen with the conversion to Christianity of the Roman emperor Constantine in 312 AD, which led to the adoption of Christianity as the state religion of the Roman Empire.

The original form of Buddhism became very much diluted and acquired not only previous incarnations of the Buddha but whole systems of bodhisattvas some of whom are, or are very close to being, gods or goddesses in their own right. These include Avalokiteshvara, who is male in India but is known as the female Guanyin in China and as Kanon in Japan where she was the Goddess of Mercy. Over the millennia of its existence Buddhism has meant rather different things to different people. However, there is no doubt that Buddha did not claim to be a god and indeed was very clear that he was a man and that he was pointing out a path to people that they would have to follow themselves.

Life after death

The belief in some form of survival after physical death is shared by many religions. The majority believe in survival in another dimension – the Underworld or Heaven and Hell – while others believe in reincarnation either as humans or animals. Reincarnation as humans has become really difficult to believe in, following the huge rise in the human population in the last few generations. Even within the Christian tradition the beliefs about the afterlife are not uniform. The mediaeval church took the view, illustrated in many representations of the Last Judgement, that the souls of the dead rested in purgatory or limbo until the Last Judgement. At this moment there is resurrection of the body as shown by the pictures of the dead rising from their graves or being disgorged from large fish or other predators. Then the sinners are consigned to hell and the good to heaven. For the present, therefore, the only inhabitants of heaven are saints and angels and the devils in hell are still waiting for their first victims! Not all modern churchmen, particularly Protestants, seem to share this view but its afterglow is sufficient to produce marked disquiet among a not insignificant part of modern European populations about the disposal of their body parts after death.

It is often speculated that a principal characteristic of the human mind (not found in other animals) is the recognition of one's own mortality – the knowledge that life is short and that we are all going to die. This may indeed be a powerful stimulus for the belief, or the wish to believe, in a continued existence after death. As quoted above, until well into the 19th century, the pattern of human mortality in towns was such that half of all children were dead before their fifth birthday, and half of the remaining population were dead by the age of 40, dying at a fairly constant rate from the age of five onwards. People therefore lived with the prospect of their own deaths and the death of those close to them as an ever-present fact of life, and great comfort must have been derived from believing that death was not final. However, the details of what to expect of life after death are usually rather unclear. Those who die old and incapacitated will presumably wish to enjoy an afterlife as children with their parents, and/or in the flower of their youth, and/or with their partner and their small children, and/or with their grandchildren – but in all cases in full possession of their faculties. To manage all these together must test the faith of even the most dedicated believers!

All religions do share one universal feature – faith or belief. The essential nature of beliefs is that they do not require any empirical evidence. The motto of the more extreme believers – for whom the term fideist will be used – is the early Christian author Tertullian's famous phrase 'Credo quia absurdum' – 'I believe because it is absurd' – probably referring to the Resurrection of Christ. This enshrines the essential nature of extreme belief. In contrast stands the view of the sceptic who will accept propositions only on the basis of evidence. The sceptics' motto is that of the Royal Society – 'Nullius in verba' – or 'Accept nothing just because someone says so' (a fairly free translation). Committed fideists and committed sceptics stand at the opposite poles of a world view and, in practice, most people, including many clerics, stand somewhere in between often moving a little one way or the other depending on the issues concerned. It is also certainly the case that much religious prescription is widely adhered to by sceptics whether or not they accept the underlying authority.

Is there a biological or genetic basis for faith versus scepticism?

It is a plausible idea that there may be some selective advantage to faith and/or to deference to authority in general, the two showing considerable concordance. Whether this trait is wholly culturally determined or has some biological basis is far from clear. On the one hand there are strongly held stereotypes of entire populations that are more or less willing to accept authoritarian rule, which would support the view that these differences are cultural. On the other there are those like Dean Hamer (2005) who consider that 'faith is hard-wired into our genes'. I am not aware of any convincing evidence for any such thing. It would require adequately powered studies of identical twins separated at birth and brought up in different faith environments even to approach this question.

There is one dominant characteristic of most, if not all, religions which cannot be explained by ideas such as a genetically determined preference for faith or acceptance of authority. This is their extreme hostility not just to other religions but to quite minor variations within a single religion. This hostility has given rise to warfare and killing on a massive scale throughout recorded history and continues to do so to this day. Believing in the same god or in the same holy scriptures provides no protection. Wars among the different variants of Christianity – Orthodox, Catholic and Protestant – and between the Sunni and Shia variants of Islam are forbidding examples. The intra-communal violence between Muslims and Hindus in India after independence is a recent example of conflict between different religions. Theologians, in my experience, tend to avoid this topic. The neo-atheists believe that it is an intrinsic characteristic of religion which they regard as a pathological aberration of human behaviour. However, if one accepts that the real function that has led to the persistence of religion is the value of its prescription as the basis of cultural evolution, then this intolerance can be seen to have a function though its extreme violence cannot.

The Spectrum Between Fideism and Scepticism

There is quite clear division in attitude between those who regard belief as central to their existence and those who are entirely sceptical of anything which does not have evidence to support it. For substantial periods of time the conflict between fideism and scepticism was predominantly focused on religion. The coming of biblical scholarship on the one hand, and the development of natural science on the other, was responsible for not only the sceptics but also many non-fideist religious believers rejecting the more literal accounts given in the holy books. The sceptical movement came to its apogee with the European Enlightenment and the recognition that experimental evidence was essential for understanding both the physical and the biological world.

In recent years, the conflict between fideism and scepticism has moved into quite different areas. Now it is by no means restricted to religion but includes such matters as genetically modified foods, vaccination, stem cell research and reproductive technologies, and these will be discussed further below. There is a powerful and well-financed movement in the UK and in Europe, and also in the United States, which rejects the Enlightenment entirely and looks back on an imagined golden pre-industrial, pre-scientific past where life was not accompanied by worries about nuclear bombs, climate change or Frankenstein foods but was also not acknowledged to have had 'No arts; no letters; no society; and which is worst of all, continual fear and danger of violent death; and the life of man, solitary, poor, nasty, brutish and short.' (Thomas Hobbes 1651).

Table 1 Prescriptions for Behaviour

	Contraception	Sexual Hygiene	Celibacy	Travel	Personal Hygiene	Worship	Moral Prescription
Buddhists	Generally permissive		Variable for monks		Prescribed	Personal devotion; occasionally at temple	Sila: to refrain from taking life; to refrain from theft; to refrain from sensual (inc. sexual) misconduct; to refrain from lying; to refrain from intoxicants
Christians	RC: natural method only. Protestants: generally permissive		Yes, for monks, nuns, RC priests			Congregational and personal devotion	The Ten Commandments; variation on many details between denominations

	Contraception	Sexual Hygiene	Celibacy	Travel	Personal Hygiene	Worship	Moral Prescription
Hindus	Permissive	Prescribed	No	Brahmins were forbidden to cross sea	Prescribed	Temple worship, personal devotion, group pilgrimage	Dharma: mercy (refusal of violence); renunciation/sense control (refusal of intoxicants); truthfulness (refusal of gambling and speculations); purity (refusal of sex forbidden in scriptures)
Jains	Permissive		Yes, for monks and nuns		Prescribed	Temple worship, personal devotion, group pilgrimage	Non-violence (Ahimsa); truth (Satya); non-stealing (Asteya); non-possission (Aparigraha)
Jews	Generally permissive	Prescribed (male circumcision)	No	Rituals prescribed for orthodox	Prescribed	Congregational and personal devotion	"Do not do unto others that which is repugnant to you" (Hillel); much variation between orthodox and reform groups

(Table 1 continued)

(Table 1 continued)

	Contraception	Sexual Hygiene	Celibacy	Travel	Personal Hygiene	Worship	Moral Prescription
Muslims	Generally permissive	Prescribed (male circumcision)	No		Prescribed	Congregational and personal devotion; Hajj	Sharia: wide-ranging prescription. Variation between different groups
Sikhs	Natural methods only	No adultery	No	Yes	Prescribed daily ablutions. No hair cutting for male or female	Personal daily prayers, morning, evening and night. Congregational sung prayers in Gurdwara	Worship one God. Follow teachings of Gurus and writings of Guru Granth Sahib. Earn an honest living. Share earnings, do public service.
Zoroastrians			No		Prescribed	Congregational and personal devotion	"Good thoughts, good words, good deeds" (Humata, Hukhta, Hvarshta); asceticism frowned upon

Table 2 Dietary Prescriptions

	Meat/Fish	Other dietary	Alcohol	Fasts
Buddhists	No	Monks can eat what they are given	No	No
Christians	Yes	Variable - RC no meat on Friday and restricted diet in Lent	Yes	Yes - occasional
Hindus	No		No	No
Jains	No	Essentially vegan	No	
Jews	Yes - only clovenhoofed ruminants or fins + scales	Kosher rules, unleavened bread	Moderation	Yes - Sabbath
Muslims	Yes - herbivores only	Hallal rules	No	Yes - Ramadan
Sikhs	Yes, in moderation. No sacrificed animals. No Kosher or Hallal meat	Eat a moderate balanced diet for health	"Do not harm body with tobacco or intoxicants". Alcohol in moderation	No. Sikhs are encouraged to cook and eat together - in the home or the Gurdwara
Zoroastrians	Yes	Eat for health	Yes	

What Bees can Tell us about the Evolution of Behaviour

My interest in the evolution of behaviour was fired by my taking up beekeeping in 1976 which the author described in 1983. This was the same year in which Richard Dawkins published *The Selfish Gene*, and one of the striking examples that he gave of altruism in animals was 'the kamikaze bee' which sacrifices its life to defend its colony. It did not take me many years of beekeeping to recognise that the kamikaze bee is a fallacy. The concept was based on the familiar observation that when bees sting human beings, who have thin elastic skins, they cannot withdraw their barbed stinger and, in trying to do so, pull out their hindgut, as a consequence of which they then die. However, bees have been in existence for hundreds of millions of years whereas Homo sapiens or the modern human, is probably some 250,000 years old. It is therefore clear that in the long evolutionary history of bees, their interactions with humans were not of major significance. Bees evolved their stings to protect their colonies against attack by other insects. When a bee stings another insect, which does not have elastic skin but has an external carapace of overlapping chitinous plates, it either drills a hole through a plate or inserts the stinger between plates and either way it seems to have no difficulty in retrieving its sting. Being a fairly unskilful beekeeper, I did from time to time allow fighting to occur between different colonies of bees and when I then examined the dead bees outside the hive they did not have their hind guts protruding and had clearly died from being stung rather than from stinging. It therefore became clear to me that not all that is written about the altruism of bee behaviour is necessarily to be taken as the definitive truth.

Bees and their behaviour

The honey bee (*Apis Mellifera*) is a species which has fascinated humans for most of their recorded history. Bees live in colonies where there are three anatomically different 'castes'. There is a single queen who is a fertile female and lays eggs, and there are the drones (fertile males) whose principal, and possibly sole, function is to mate with a virgin queen on her mating flight, although it is possible that they also serve a more mundane function in helping to keep the hive warm at certain times of the year. The third caste is the infertile females (or workers) who do everything else. There are clearly some analogies here to human societies although one should be careful not to overstate this. Generally received wisdom assumes that the queen controls the workers, but beekeepers know that it is the other way around. However, the observation that bees appear to behave altruistically has long been of interest to evolutionary biologists (not all of whom seem to be particularly familiar with bees) who regarded altruism as a puzzling feature of natural selection.

The honey bee uses a survival strategy that is unusual in insects. Probably almost alone of insects in temperate climates honey bees overwinter the whole colony rather than overwintering only the queen, which is the custom with wasps and most other insects. Because honey bees overwinter the whole colony, they have a need for ample supplies of food to provide the colony with a source of energy when there is no forage for them. The reason for this is that, while the individual bee has no mechanism for keeping itself warm, the cluster of bees which forms the overwintering colony does keep itself warm, at about 35o Centigrade by metabolising honey. The cluster is not quiescent but the bees that are outside gradually circulate so that they go inside and then outside again. This means that the whole cluster is able to maintain a constant temperature. When spring comes, bees again need stores not only of honey but also of pollen, in order to raise their brood to build up a colony of adequate size to take advantage of the foraging. It is because of their storage of large quantities of honey that they have been of major interest to humans for most of human history. Eva Crane, in her classic 1983 work on the archaeology of beekeeping is of the opinion that the robbing of bees' nests to collect honey is one of the oldest human activities and can be seen depicted in prehistoric cave paintings. This form of honey gathering still persists in some parts of the world. Certainly the keeping of bees by humans under artificial conditions, originally in skeps and later in hives, also goes back at least some millennia and Virgil, for example, wrote about it. However, true understanding of how bee colonies operate had to wait until the 19th century and indeed more recently than that for a proper understanding.

The reproductive mechanisms of bees are rather different from those with which we are familiar in mammals. The queen is derived from a fertilised egg and is therefore diploid[3]. She differs from other workers in having been fed royal jelly as a grub and is therefore larger and becomes sexually mature in a way that worker bees, who are sterile, diploid females, do not. When the queen is hatched she will, if there is a queen still present in a hive, kill the older queen or attempt to do so. Frequently, however, the old queen with part of the hive colony will already have left the hive to find a new home. This is known as swarming and is how bee colonies reproduce The newly hatched virgin queen then goes on a mating flight during which she is fertilised by drones flying in the same area. These drones, in the process of mating, deposit large numbers of sperm in a specialised organ, the spermatheca,. The sperm will derive from up to 20 different drones encountered on the mating flight. There are in the region of five million sperm stored at the end of one mating flight, which last the queen for her whole reproductive life of two years or so, during which she lays between 1,000 and 2,000 eggs a day. Fertilisation of an ovum takes place only after the egg is laid. It is the workers who determine whether an egg laid by the queen is fertilised or not and this depends on the shape and size of the cell which they build for the queen to lay into. If the cell is narrow, which it commonly is, the queen, in order to lay an egg, has to bend her thorax or abdomen, which allows a sperm to be laid along with the egg. Fertilisation then occurs in the bottom of the cell before

---

[3] Diploid describes organisms where each cell has two sets of chromosomes, one of each pair being derived from each parent. Haploid describes organisms that have a single set of chromosomes. In mammals, only the ova and sperm are haploid and all other cells are diploid.

the nurse bees (young workers) fill it with pollen-derived material and seal it so that a grub can develop. If they build larger cells the queen does not have to bend her abdomen and the egg will not be fertilised, and from these cells the males, the haploid drones, will develop.

This curious genetic process leads to the offspring of one drone and one queen being 75 per cent related to each other rather than the 50 per cent relationship found among normal siblings with two diploid parents. The recognition that in these particular circumstances bees are 75 per cent genetically identical was used as an explanation by sociobiologists Edward Wilson in 1975 and Richard Dawkins in 1976, who claimed that altruism could be explained on the basis of kin selection. However, the idea that all the bees in a hive are the progeny of a single queen and a single drone is a charming fallacy all of its own. It had been held – without any real evidence – that when the virgin queen goes on her mating flight she mates only with the fastest and most active drone, providing in this way an excellent example of sexual selection. It was only the sperm of this one drone that filled the spermatheca of the queen with spermatozoa. However, once it became possible to film the mating flights of bee queens, something which required the technological developments of the second half of the 20th century, it became apparent that this idea was entirely incorrect and that the queen flies through drone congregation areas – where drones from many colonies aggregate for reasons that are not fully understood – and mates with every available drone. Furthermore, since the spermatheca is of limited size, it is probable that there is over-representation of the drones she mates with towards the end of her mating flight rather than the beginning, so that the idea that there is a great race for producing the next generation taking place during the mating flights is also unlikely to be true. It is therefore certainly the case that the workers in a single colony of bees originate from a number of different drones and that the workers will not be 75 per cent genetically identical.

Furthermore, the whole idea that bees sense their kin relationship and that this promotes their so-called altruistic behaviour is itself known by any beekeeper to be quite untrue. It is a common practice in beekeeping when one has two colonies, neither of which is particularly strong, to unite them. This is done by placing one colony over the other, separated by a piece of newspaper in which tiny pinpricks are made, so that by the time the bees come into close contact with each other they have got used to the 'smell' of pheromones from the other colony and do not recognise them as foreign. If there are two queens present, one will kill the other and there will only be one queen left in the united colony. This united colony will be made up of roughly equivalent numbers of bees of entirely different genetic origins and yet such a colony defends its hive against attacks by other insects in exactly the same way as a colony which has not been united in this way. Again, the idea that kin selection explains the behaviour in bees in defending their hives is a pleasing thought that is totally contrary to the evidence provided by everyday beekeeping.

A great deal of confusion has therefore arisen from the social organisation of bees and the genetics of bee behaviour. However, the opponents of group selection could never quite make up their mind whether a colony of bees should be considered as a single entity since it has only one fertile reproducing individual or whether the individual worker bees should be regarded as individuals who behave altruistically in working for the good of the hive and in defending it against attackers. Neither attitude provides a convincing argument against group selection. Nor do they account for altruism, which is at the basis of the arguments about group selection. There is, however, one aspect of regarding a colony of bees as the analogue of a moral community of humans which does have a major implication for evolutionary biology. This is the re-queening phenomenon.

The re-queening phenomenon

Bees, like humans, live in communities where co-operation between individuals performing different tasks is essential for survival. The honey bee colony consists, as already described, of one queen, a number of drones and a large population of workers. The drones mate with a virgin queen on her mating flight and possibly have some function in keeping the hives warm, but otherwise do little. The workers do everything else. They nurse the larvae, they build the wax cells, they keep the hive clean and they forage for nectar and pollen, and the efficiency with which they do this, and some other characteristics such as their level of aggressiveness, vary from colony to colony. When beekeepers have a colony whose behaviour seems unfavourable – if the bees are untidy builders and cappers, if they are aggressive, if they are lazy and if they are prone to swarming – they may choose to change this by introducing a newly mated queen from a better-behaved colony into his hive. This is done very frequently and the effect is always the same. The bees that emerge from the eggs laid by the new queen behave entirely in accord with their genetic background. They learn nothing from the bees among whom they grow up. This re-queening experiment shows beyond doubt that these variations in bee behaviour are genetically determined even if we do not yet understand which genes are involved. For this reason bees have no need for religions!

Experiments analogous to the re-queening experiment have frequently been done in humans and give precisely the opposite result. Robert Fitzroy and Charles Darwin possibly did the first experiment of this kind in taking several natives from Patagonia back to the United Kingdom. The three survivors were taken back to Patagonia to encourage European civilisation there, apparently with no success (Thompson 2015). However, there is no doubt that experiments of moving children by adoption from one culture to another, which are now very common, have demonstrated that the behavioural variation that distinguishes different groups is not genetically determined but entirely cultural. Such children grow up with the behavioural characteristics of their adoptive families rather than those of their genetic ancestors. It is because human behavioural variation is culturally determined that I have argued that humans need religion.

Genetic Engineering

In 1953 Watson and Crick published their double helix structure for DNA from which the mechanism of DNA replication was readily deduced and led on to the sequencing of DNA and eventually of whole genomes. However, it was not until the 1970s that a number of new discoveries – in apparently unrelated fields – came together to allow the manipulation of genes. (This is often called 'recombinant DNA technology' or 'genetic engineering'.) These were the discovery of: bacterial plasmids – the DNA-containing particles that transfer genetic material (for example genes coding for antibiotic resistance) between bacteria; 'restriction endonucleases' – bacterial enzymes that clip DNA with sequence specificity; and 'reverse transcriptase' – a viral enzyme that copies RNA back into DNA, which is necessary for the replication of some viruses. By making use of these three discoveries it became possible to clone and to manipulate genes. At first the technology was quite difficult and time-consuming, but technical advances, notably a chemical way of reproducing DNA by the 'polymerase chain reaction' in the early 1980s, allowed its widespread use in biology and medicine.

Advances in this area have been extensive and rapid and show no signs of slowing down. Fideists tend to be highly suspicious of genetic engineering in general and regard it as humans taking over activities that they regard as falling within the remit of the divine.

Nevertheless many applications of genetic engineering in medicine are well established and not at all controversial. These include the recombinant protein vaccine against Hepatitis B, which has been hugely successful in reducing the incidence of this important disease and in preventing many cases of liver cancer. Because the earlier plasma-derived vaccine always carried the danger of contamination with unknown viruses, the recombinant vaccine is much to be preferred both on the grounds of safety and efficacy. Another example is the use of recombinant growth hormone to treat children with dwarfism due to its deficiency. Since the growth hormone extracted from human pituitary glands was able to transmit Creutzfeld Jacob Disease, the new recombinant product was very welcome.

The first application of genetic engineering to food was 'vegetarian cheese'. Strict vegetarians object to eating hard cheese because in its production milk is first curdled with rennet, an enzyme derived from calf's stomach which involves killing the calf. To avoid using rennet, cheese manufacturers started using chymase, an enzyme made from genetically engineered yeast, instead. This was accepted without any opposition. The first genetically modified food plant was the 'FlavrSavr' tomato, which has a genetic modification (an antisense polygalacturonase) to delay softening. It was introduced to the market rather cautiously and was also accepted apparently without controversy.

The ongoing furore about genetically modified food crops (GMOs) had its origins in the introduction of two genetically modified commodity crops by Monsanto, and particularly by their (unwise) introduction into unmodified crops so that the consumers would not know whether the product contained genetically modified material. The two introduced genes (or transgenes) involved were:

1. A gene that makes a plant resistant to the herbicide glyphosate, which can then be used to kill the weeds in the crop. Oil seed rape and soya were modified in this way.
2. The *Bacillus thuringiensis* toxin, which confers resistance to stem-boring insects. (This toxin is used in organic agriculture when applied as a spray of whole bacteria.) Maize was modified in this way.

These introductions were not well received! A coalition of those opposed to corporate agriculture and to big business as a whole joined with those opposed to science as a whole and those worried particularly about genetics and 'playing God'; others, not least in the media, saw an opportunity for publicity and gain, and a group of maverick scientists – now inevitably involved in any media controversy about science – instituted a campaign to persuade the public that GMOs were a conspiracy against poor farmers, a fraud on the gullibility of those farmers who grow them, an intrinsic evil and a hazard to human health and the environment.

None of this bears inspection. All plant breeding involves genetic manipulation. Many varieties have been derived from irradiated seeds which can give multiple and undesirable changes. All novel plant varieties produced for food need rigorous testing for toxicity, allergenicity and possible effects on the environment. The techniques of plant breeding made possible by modern molecular biology are simply techniques and raise no ethical issues that are different from any other form of plant breeding.

At a time when climate change is justifiably a matter of huge concern it is extraordinary that the Green movement still rejects the genetic modification of plants. If one could increase the efficiency of photosynthesis from one per cent as it is now to five per cent this would allow all the energy needs of the planet to be met from land now under cultivation as described by Lord Porter in 1995. Even smaller improvements, which would be easier to achieve, would make a major difference.

It is only now in 2019 when the consequences of global warming have become inescapably obvious that some signs of change in their position are appearing but the European Union continues to ban all GMO foods.

Church and State

With the coming of the Enlightenment and with the growth of the secular state, and increasingly the separation of Church and State in a number of advanced Western countries, the relationship between Church and State has become more complex. In many areas of behaviour one relies on secular laws to determine what is not allowed. However, the ethical paradigm on which eventually the laws are based has not changed that much and does still reflect the religious prescriptions that have been in place for a very long time. This can, of course, be seen to produce a considerable problem because of the difficulty of changing the prescription to meet changed circumstances. The obvious situation that occurs relates to the increase of numbers. The prescription in most existing religions attaches the greatest importance to increasing population numbers and to protecting the right to breed. This is not, of course, entirely unfettered but nevertheless is regarded as a fundamental human right. However, we now live in a world where it is widely agreed that human over-population is extremely damaging to the resources of the planet and that any further growth in human numbers is likely to have highly disadvantageous effects on many other species, and indeed on humans themselves. It has nevertheless proved extremely difficult to move towards the new ethical prescription which attaches more importance to restricting the population than to expanding numbers.

Surprisingly, with the growth of electronic means of communication (though possibly not due to this fact) another very disturbing trend has come to light since the end of the Second World War. This is an articulate and highly assertive movement that rejects the Enlightenment altogether and looks back towards a vision of a golden, wholly imaginary, past in which religion provided ethical certainty and science and technology did not interfere with deeply held views of how things were to be. This anti-rational movement is quite widespread and concentrates on a whole variety of topics, moving all the way from interference with reproductive techniques to genetic modification of plants for food use, to alternative medicine, to vaccines, to organic food, etc. The argument often advanced by such groups is that they reject activities which they do not regard as natural. This is, however, not a satisfactory approach since a definition of what is to be regarded as natural is not usually advanced. At the most fundamental end, they would probably regard as natural only those activities that are entirely without human agency. However, since this would involve not wearing clothes and not eating cooked food, one can be confident that even the most fundamentalist of the anti-Enlightenment group are not prepared to take it anything like that far. If one tries to get some definition of what may be considered natural and unnatural from religious teaching, that is also quite difficult. Religions are more likely to express opinions on what they regard as being against nature rather than unnatural. The current furore in the Anglican Church about homosexuality is a good example. A substantial proportion of the Anglican Church regard homosexuality as against nature, but it is certainly not unnatural in the sense defined above, since homosexuality is found in species other than humans. It is possible, I suppose, to look for a definition from patent law, which distinguishes between discoveries which are not patentable and inventions which are. This again is based on the fact that an invention must involve some original and novel human contribution. Again, however, it is difficult to imagine many people who would be prepared not to make use of anything that has ever been granted a patent. This would deprive one of all the conveniences of modern life and most medical care. One really has to admit that there is no objective definition of what is natural or unnatural and what is actually in use are declamatory definitions, i.e. this is unnatural because I say it is unnatural. That, of course, is essentially extremely unhelpful since peoples' views on this will be extremely variable.

Conclusion

The model that has been described from the functions of religions as providing building blocks for competing models of cultural evolution between human moral communities can be seen to have served humans well over long periods of time. During all these ages, however, the problems tackled by cultural evolution were to some extent local, so the different human moral communities could operate in different ways and thereby compete. However, in the last two centuries or so, and certainly more recently, it has become clear that there are problems with which this model cannot adequately cope. This is because of the enormous expansion of the human population, which has led to problems on a global scale which cannot adequately be addressed by the different competing ways of different human moral communities. The most obvious current example is climate change: the enormous increase in the emission of greenhouse gases is producing changes that affect the whole planet and which, if not controlled in some unified fashion, are very likely to produce changes of a catastrophic nature which could render considerable areas of the planet uninhabitable. Similarly, the disposal of waste, and particularly plastic waste, has become a global problem that requires a co-operative global solution. It may also be that the planet cannot in the long-term support more than a certain sized human population which we may already be close to exceeding. That is not certain, as technical improvements in the use of energy and improved methods of growing food may still cope with this problem for the foreseeable future. It is, however, amply clear that what is needed in the modern world is a co-operative approach to solving world problems. It is unfortunately equally clear that passionate adherents to individual, often quite closely related religions, continue to make such a collaborative approach increasingly difficult. It does seem an inescapable conclusion that many decisions affecting the whole world need to be made at a secular level on the basis of scientific knowledge and rational argument, and that the co-operative approach is of course at total variance with the traditional way that competing religions have worked. There is sadly no indication at the present time that the world is progressing in a rational direction. Indeed, the reverse seems to be the case. It is, of course, unwise to project into the future the consequences of current trends continuing in the same depressing way as the last 10 years have shown, but it is fair to say that if ecological disaster is to be avoided the world will need to come to terms with scientific reality rather than the concept based on holy books that are thousands of years old. It could certainly help if fideists of all religions could accept that, just as sex should be confined to consenting adults in private, so religion should be confined to worshipping their god(s) on the relevant day of the week and should not define their secular existence. This is not so far from Christ's injunction to 'Render therefore unto Caesar the things which are Caesar's; and unto God the things that are God's' that it should be impossible to achieve but there is again no sign at all of any progress in this direction in the first two decades of the present millennium.

Acknowledgements

The contributions of Sylvia Lachmann in researching and preparing the tables of religious prescriptions, and of Barbara King for invaluable secretarial assistance, are gratefully acknowledged.

This publication is based on and extends a number of previously published papers:

Lachmann, P.J. Why religions? An evolutionary view of the behaviour of bees and men. Cambridge Rev 1983; 104: 22–26.

Lachmann, P.J. God 'To be or not to be; that is *not* the question'. Amer J Psychology 2009; Summer, 272–278.

Lachmann, P.J. Genetic and cultural evolution: From fossils to proteins; and from behaviour to ethics. European Review 2010a; 18(3): 297–309.

Lachmann, P.J. Religion – An evolutionary adaptation. The FASEB Journal 2010b; 24: 1301–1307.

Lachmann, P.J. Ethics evolve. European Review 2013; 21: S109–S113.

Lachmann, P.J. Evolution, ethics and religion. Global Bioethics 2014; 25:3: 156–163

References

Attenborough, D. *Life on Earth: A Natural History*. William Collins & Sons, London, 1979.

Avery, O.T., Macleod, C.M., McCarty, M., Studies on the chemical nature of the substance inducing transformation of pneumococcal types: induction of transformation by a desoxyribonucleic acid fraction isolated from pneumococcus type III. J Exp Med 1944; 79(2): 137–158.

Bonner, J.T. *The evolution of culture in animals*. Princeton University Press, New Jersey, 1980.

Brenner S https://www.youtube.com/watch?v=bFku7siFdsY 2017

Cairns, J. *Matters of life and death: perspectives on public health, molecular biology, cancer and the prospects for the human race.* Princeton University Press, New Jersey, 1997.

Cornford, F.M. *Microcosmographia Academica* Chapter VII, 2nd Edition, Bowes and Bowes, Cambridge, 1922.

Costeloe, K., Hennessy, E., Gibson, A.T., Marlow, N., Wilkinson, A.R. The EPICure Study: Outcomes to Discharge from Hospital for Infants Born at the Threshold of Viability. Pediatrics 2000; 106: 659–671.

Coulson, S.D. World's oldest ritual discovered. Worship the python 70,000 years ago. Apollon 30 Nov 2006, University of Oslo, Norway. http://www.apollon.uio.no/english/articles/2006/python-english.html

Cowan, M. https://www.prospectmagazine.co.uk/magazine/edward-wilson-social-conquest-earth-evolutionary-errors-origin-species

Crane, E. *The Archaeology of Beekeeping*. Duckworth, London, 1983.

Darwin, C. *The Origin Of Species By Means Of Natural Selection* 6th Edition. John Murray, London, 1873.

Dawkins, R. *The Selfish Gene.* Oxford University Press, Oxford, 1976.

Dawkins, R. The Extended Phenotype. Oxford University Press, Oxford, 1982.

Dawkins, R. *The God Delusion.* Houghton Mifflin, Boston, 2006.

Dawkins, R. The Descent of Edward Wilson. *Prospect Magazine,* June 2012.

De Waal, F. *The Bonobo and the Atheist: In Search of Humanism among the Primates.* W.W. Norton & Co., New York, 2013.

Diamond, J. *Collapse: how societies choose to fail or succeed.* Penguin Books, London, 2005.

Dolhenty, J. An Overview of Natural Law. Radical Academy.org 2012.

Ganesh, K. Neuberger, M.S., The relationship between hypothesis and experiment in unveiling the mechanisms of antibody gene diversification. FASEB J. 2011 Apr; 25(4): 1123–1132.

Griffith, F. The significance of pneumococcal types. J. Hygiene 1928; 27(2): 113–159.

Hamer, D.H. *The God Gene: how faith is hardwired into our genes.* Anchor Books, New York, 2005.

Hamilton, W.D. The evolution of altruistic behavior. American Naturalist 1963; 97(896): 354–356.

Hawking, S., Mlodinow, L. *The Grand Design.* Transworld Ltd., London, 2011.

Henshilwood, C.S., d'Errico, F., van Niekerk, K.L., Coquinot, Y., Jacobs, Z., Lauritzen, S-E., Menu, M., Garcia-Morena, R.A. 100,000-year-old ochre-processing workshop at Blombos Cave, South Africa. Science 14 Oct 2011; 334: 219–222.

Hitchins, C. *God is Not Great.* Atlantic, London, 2007.

Hobbes, T. *Leviathan.* Republished by Penguin Classics, London, 2016.

Huxley, T.H. Evolution and Ethics. Ethics and evolution. Collected essays Vol. 9. Macmillan, London, 1893.

Johnson, S.A. *Dictionary of the English Language.* 6th Edition. Peacock and Sons, London 1806.

Johnston, C. Biological warfare flares up again between E.O. Wilson and Richard Dawkins. US scientist dismisses Dawkins as a 'journalist' in a BBC television interview about pair's differing views on natural selection. *the Guardian,* 7 Nov 2014.

Kant I, Groundwork of the Metaphysics of Morals (1785)

Kellett, E.E. *A Short History of Religions* Chapter 1. Victor Gollancz Ltd., London, 1933.

Kenny, A. The Essence of Morality. European Review 2013; 21(S1): S123–S126.

Lachmann, P.J. Why Religions? An evolutionary view of the behaviour of bees and men. Cambridge Review 1983; 104: 22–26.

Lachmann, P.J. The amplification loop of the complement pathways (Section II). Adv Imm 2009; 104: 115–148.

Lachmann, P.J. The Grandmother effect. Gerontology 2011; 57: 375–377.

Lachmann, P.J. The influence of infection on society. In: The freedom of scientific research. Giordano, S., Harris, J. and Piccirillo, L. Eds. Manchester University Press, Manchester, 2019.

Larroque, B., Ancel, P.Y., Marret, S., Marchand, L., André, M., Arnaud, C., Pierrat, V., Rozé, J.C., Messer, J., Thiriez, G., Burguet, A., Picaud, J.C., Bréart, G., Kaminski, M. Eurodevelopmental disabilities and special care of 5-year-old children born before 33 weeks of gestation (the EPIPAGE study): a longitudinal cohort study. Lancet 2008; 371: 813–820.

Loudon, I. *Death in childbirth. An international study of maternal care and maternal mortality 1800–1950.* Clarendon Press, Oxford, 1992.

o   Macfarlane Robert Gwyn General introduction to Discussion on triggered enzyme cascades of Blood Plasma *Proc. R. Soc. Lond. B* **173 1969**

o   Mendel, J.G. 'Versuche über Pflanzenhybriden', Verhandlungen des naturforschenden Vereines in Brünn, Bd. IV für das Jahr, 1865, Abhandlungen: 3–47. For the English translation, see: Druery, C.T., Bateson, Experiments in plant hybridization. Journal of the Royal Horticultural Society 1901; 26: 1–32.

Norenzayan, A. *Big Gods: How Religion Transformed Cooperation and Conflict.* Princeton University Press, New Jersey, 2013.

Ohno, S. Evolution by gene duplication. Allen and Unwin, Crow's Nest, New South Wales, 1970.

Oldstone-Moore, J. *Confucianism.* Oxford University Press, Oxford, 2002.

Orgel, L.E. *Origins of Life: Molecules and Natural Selection.* Chapman & Hall, London, 1973.

Popper, K.R. Logik der Forschung first published 1935 by Verlag von Julius Springer, Vienna, Austria First English edition published 1959 by Hutchinson & Co. First published by Routledge 1992 First published in Routledge Classics 2002 by Routledge 11 New Fetter Lane, London EC4P 4EE

Porter, G. Life under the sun. Rajiv Ghandhi Science and Technology Lecture, Pune, India. 9 Jan 1995.

Rees, M.J. *Our Cosmic Habitat.* Orion Publishing Group, London, 2001.

Richards, E.J. Inherited epigenetic variation – revisiting soft inheritance. Nat Rev Genet. 2006 May; 7(5): 395–401.

Rosenberg, K.R. The evolution of modern human childbirth. American Journal of Physical Anthropology. 1992; 35(S15): 89–124.

Royal Society. Population, the complex reality: a report of the population summit of the world's scientific academies. Conference Proceedings of the Population Summit 1993, New Delhi, India. Graham-Smith, F. Ed. London, Royal Society, 1994. http://www.interacademies.org/13940/IAP-Statement-on-Population-Growth

Sainsbury, A.W., Deaville, R., Lawson, B., Cooley, W.A., Farelly, S.S.J., Stack, M.J., Duff, P., McInnes, C.J., Gurnell, J., Russell, P.H., Rushton, S.P., Pfeiffer, D.U., Nettleton, P., Lurz, P. Poxviral disease in red squirrels *Sciurus vulgaris* in the UK: spatial and temporal trends of an emerging threat. EcoHealth 2008; 5: 305–316.

Sedley, D. *Creationism and its critics in antiquity.* University of California Press, Oakland, CA, 2007.

Spencer, H. *Principles of Biology.* Williams and Norgate, London, 1864.

Stenger, V.J. *God: The Failed Hypothesis. How science shows that God does not exist.* Prometheus, New York, 2007.

Stringer, C.B. *The Origin of Our Species*. Allen Lane, London, 2011.

Stringer, C. The origin and evolution of Homo sapiens. Philos Trans R Soc Lond B Biol Sci. 2016 Jul 5;371(1698). pii: 20150237.

Takahashi, K. and Yanamaka, S. Induction of pluripotent stem cells from mouse embryonic and adult fibroblast cultures by defined factors. Cell 2006; 126: 663–676.

Takei, K., Nakamura, K. Archaeal diversity and community development in deep-sea hydrothermal vents. Current Opin in Microbiology 2001; 14: 282–291.

Tollefsbol, Trygve Handbook of Epigenetics: The New Molecular and Medical Genetics. Elsevier Science. (2017). p. 234. ISBN 978-0-12-805477-2. Originally published in Weismann's 1889 Essays Upon Heredity

Thompson Harry This thing of Darkness Hachette 2005

Watson, J.D., Crick, F.H. Molecular structure of nucleic acids: a structure for deoxyribose nucleic acid. Nature 1953; 171(4356): 737–738.

Weismann, A. The Germ-Plasm: A Theory of Heredity. 1893. The Electronic Scholarly Publishing Project. http://www.esp.org/books/weismann/germ-plasm/facsimile/

Wetlaufer, D.B. Nucleation, rapid folding, and globular intrachain regions in proteins. Proc Natl Acad Sci USA 1973; 70: 697–701.

Williams, G.C. *Adaptation in Natural Selection*. Princeton University Press, New Jersey, 1996.

Wilmut, I., Schnieke, A.E., McWhir, J., Kind, A.J., Campbell, K.H. Viable offspring derived from foetal and adult mammalian cells. Nature 1997; 385: 810–813.

Wilson, D.S., Wilson, E.O. Rethinking the theoretical foundation of sociobiology. Quart Rev Biol. 2007; 82(4): 327–348.

Wilson, D.S. Richard Dawkins, Edward O. Wilson and the consensus of the many. Evolution Institute. 1 Jan 2015. https://evolution-institute.org/richard-dawkins-edward-o-wilson-and-the-consensus-of-the-many/

Wilson, E.O. *Sociobiology: The New Synthesis*. Harvard University Press, Cambridge, Mass., 1975.

Wilson, E.O. *The Social Conquest of the Earth*. Norton, New York, 2012.

About the author

Sir Peter Lachmann ScD (Cantab) FRCP FRCPath FRS
FMedSci

Emeritus Sheila Joan Smith Professor of Immunology,
University of Cambridge.

Peter Lachmann trained in biochemistry and medicine at
Cambridge and University College Hospital graduating
in 1956.

He was the founder President of the UK Academy of
Medical Sciences (1998-2002), Biological secretary of
the Royal Society (1993 –98) and President of the Royal
College of Pathologists (1990-93); and served on
UNESCO's international bioethics committee from
1993-98. In these capacities he has become involved
with the ethical and policy aspects of medical science.

He has kept bees for over 30 years and this hobby
combined with his professional interest in molecular
evolution has fostered his interest in cultural evolution,
ethics and religion.